PIXAR
MUSEUM
STORIES AND ART FROM THE ANIMATION STUDIO

A STUDIO PRESS BOOK

First published in the UK in 2021 by Studio Press,
an imprint of Bonnier Books UK Limited,
4th Floor, Victoria House,
Bloomsbury Square,
London
WC1B 4DA

www.bonnierbooks.co.uk

1 3 5 7 9 10 8 6 4 2

ISBN 978-1-78741-657-4

Written by Simon Beecroft
Edited by Sophie Blackman
Designed by Rob Ward
Production by Emma Kidd

A CIP catalogue for this book is available from the British Library
Printed and bound in Italy

Front cover, clockwise from top: WALL•E and EVE lighting study by John Lee;
Mr Incredible, digital art by Paul Rogers; Mike and Sulley, gouache digital art
by Ricky Nierva and Dice Tsutsumi; Nemo character study in pastel by Ralph
Eggleston; *Cars* pastel art by Bill Cone; Woody and Bo Peep digital art by John Lee.

Back cover, clockwise from top: Merida acrylic and digital artwork by Steve Pilcher; *Up*
character art, gouache on board by Ricky Nierva; Miguel digital art by Ernesto Nemesio with
layout by Robert Kondo; Remy digital art by Harley Jessup with layout by Enrico Casarosa.

WELCOME TO THE PIXAR MUSEUM

STORIES AND ART FROM THE ANIMATION STUDIO

1: *Mr Incredible*
A striking poster representing the golden era of Supers, created for the wall of magazine covers and news clippings that Bob Parr keeps in his office. Digital art by Paul Rogers.

PIXAR MUSEUM

PREFACE

1: **Rat run**

The light-drenched tourist attractions of Paris are contrasted with the shadowy presence of rat siblings Remy and Emile in this digital concept painting from *Ratatouille*, by Robert Kondo.

Story is crucial: this is the golden rule of Pixar Animation Studios. Story drives every decision made by our filmmakers, along with the belief that every pixel of every shot in one of our films should contribute to telling the story. For more than thirty-five years, Pixar has created films that have explored universal truths. These movies have captured the imaginations of audiences young and old, across the globe. Pixar strives to tell stories that so many of us can relate to in our own lives. While the characters on the screen may be toys, monsters, cars, or fish, the stories are all rooted in a deeply human experience.

The team at Pixar creates immersive cinematic experiences by imagining – and putting onscreen – authentic, vibrant worlds. For each film, characters and sets are painstakingly crafted and brought to life by artists in each department of the studio. This book invites you to delve into the fascinating work of these individuals. From concept art to storyboards and colour scripts, you'll discover a curated art collection showcasing Pixar's animated feature films and shorts.

Audiences love our films because they form an emotional connection with the stories that we tell. It is our hope that such a connection enables the audience to embark on a deeper adventure, to empathise with the characters, and even to understand a little bit more about themselves. When this happens, a film becomes something larger than itself to them. It becomes a part of their memory and experience – part of their story.

In many ways, this book is the story of how we make our films. I hope that it sheds some light on our process and how we strive to create art with tremendous impact. I now welcome you to turn the page and begin your journey into the wondrous worlds of Pixar…

Jay Ward
Pixar Animation Studios, Creative Director of Franchise

1: ***Heroes' welcome***
Flik returns to the ant colony with the troupe of circus performers that he has mistaken for warriors. Concept artwork for *A Bug's Life* in acrylics by Tia W. Kratter, layout by Geefwee Boedoe.

1: *Underwater cliff*

On the edge of their coral reef home, Nemo and his parents are reduced to specks by the size and scale of the open ocean. Mark Whiting, acrylic.

SECTION 1

ENTRANCE

It all started with a computer scientist, an animator, and an entrepreneur. Together they founded a company that changed the face of animation. From its home in the Bay Area of California, Pixar Animation Studios continues to go from strength to strength.

IN THE BEGINNING

Pixar Animation Studios' origins start as far back as the 1970s, when computer animation was in its infancy. In 1979, *Star Wars* director George Lucas hired Ed Catmull to create a Computer Division at Lucasfilm.[1] Catmull had graduated from the University of Utah in Computer Science and, after graduation, he worked as the director of the Computer Graphics Laboratory at the New York Institute of Technology. At Lucasfilm, Catmull ran the entire Computer Division, which created computer-animated elements for some live-action films, such as *Star Trek II: The Wrath of Khan* and *Star Wars: Episode VI – Return of the Jedi*.

In 1984, Catmull hired John Lasseter, who shared Catmull's belief that computer animation had a future. Lasseter and Alvy Ray Smith, along with a small team in the Computer Division, created Lucasfilm's first piece of character-based computer animation, a short called *The Adventures of André & Wally B.* The story follows a bee named Wally B. as he chases after a character named André. The story ends with both a sting and a bent stinger. Though about six seconds of the film was incomplete, it premiered in July in Minneapolis at SIGGRAPH, an annual computer graphics conference. The final version released in August at Toronto's International Animation Festival.

In 1986, the co-founder of Apple Computer Company, Steve Jobs, acquired Lucasfilm's Computer Division, which was renamed Pixar after its most well-known product: a high-end computer called the Pixar Image Computer, which the team had developed a few years earlier. Initially, Pixar focused on selling the Pixar Image Computer to specialised businesses such as medical research firms, intelligence agencies, and graphic arts companies, including Walt Disney Studios.

1

3

KEY TO PLATE

1: ***The three founders***
Pixar was founded by three men with different, but highly complementary, talents: Ed Catmull, a computer scientist; Steve Jobs, an entrepreneur, and John Lasseter, a Disney-trained animator. Depicted here in sketches by Teddy Newton.

2: ***The Adventures of André & Wally B.***
This short film was the first 3D animated film to feature simulated motion blur – the slight blurring of objects in movement – adding to the feeling of realistic motion. Concept/direction by Alvy Ray Smith, character design and animation by John Lasseter.

3: ***Red's Dream***
Pixar's second animated short film, which was released in 1987, was a moody, atmospheric piece about an unloved unicycle who dreams of a better life.

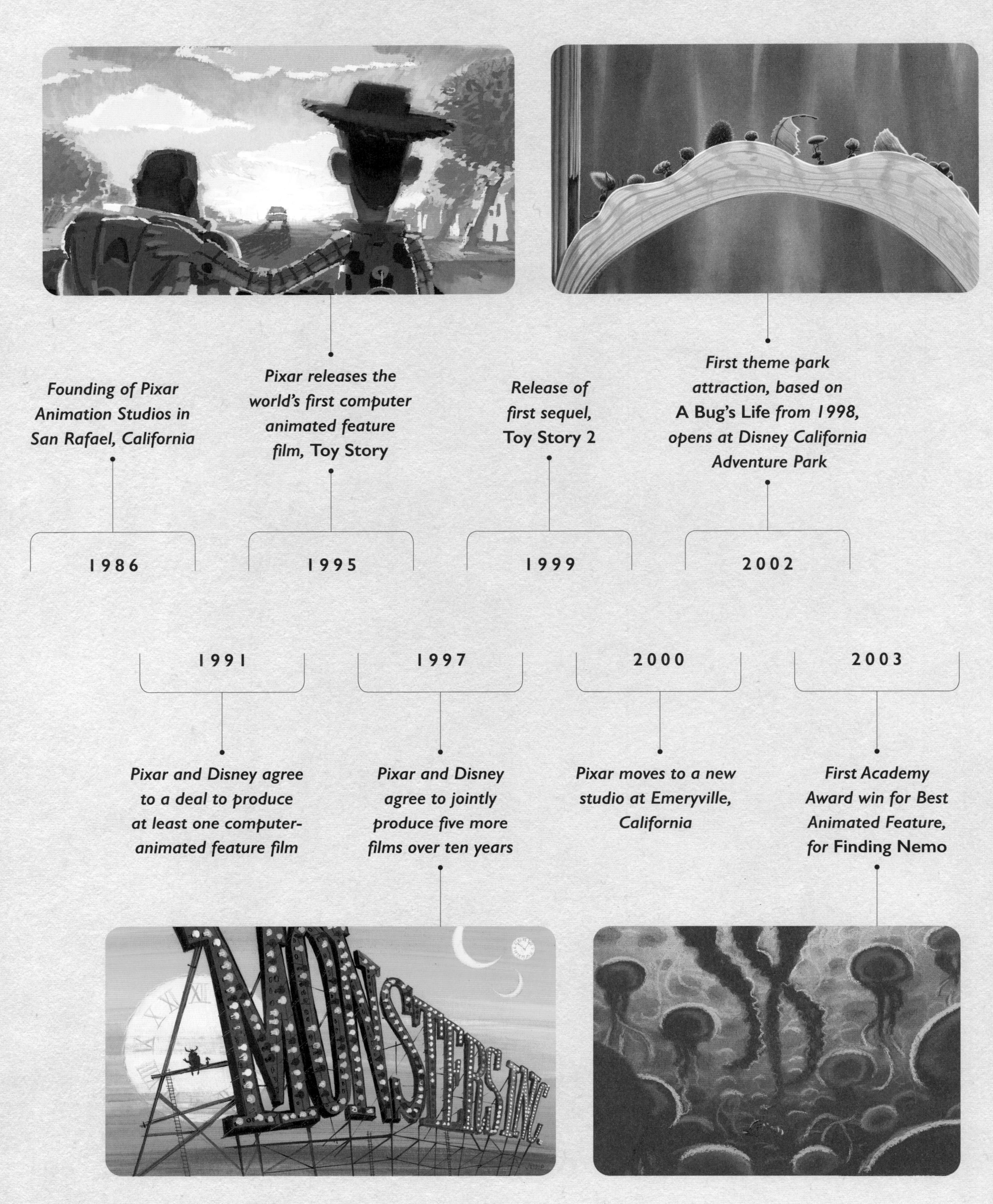

Top left, see page 19; top right, see page 39;
bottom left, see page 27; bottom right, see page 41.

2005

First exhibition of original artwork, Pixar: 20 Years of Animation, opens at the Museum of Modern Art in New York

2006

Pixar celebrates 20th anniversary, releases Cars, *and Disney acquires Pixar*

2009

First time a Pixar film was nominated for the Academy Award for Best Picture, for Up

2011

*Celebrates 25th anniversary; releases first non-*Toy Story *sequel,* Cars 2

2013

First TV special, Toy Story of Terror

2018

Incredibles 2 *becomes Pixar's biggest grossing movie and the third biggest animated movie of all time*

2020

Completion of Soul, *the first film Pete Doctor directed since becoming Pixar's Chief Creative Officer in 2018*

2021

Luca *becomes Pixar's second film, after* Soul, *to be premiered on Disney+ due to COVID-19*

Top left, see page 43; top right, see page 35;
bottom left, see page 52; bottom right, see page 51.

THE HOUSE OF PIXAR

When the group that would become Pixar was part of Lucasfilm's Computer Division, their office was on Kerner Boulevard in San Rafael, a town in Marin County, north of San Francisco. When Steve Jobs bought the company in 1986, they moved to their own office just across the street. When the lease came up in 1990, Pixar rented a larger space in an office park beside an industrial area in a small town called Point Richmond in the East Bay. They had one indulgence here: a screening room. They couldn't afford built-in seats so employees donated old sofas and armchairs. The animators also brought in old scooters and raced around the corridors, competitively scribbling a league table of best race times on the wall. The animators decorated their cubicles with some elaborate themes, such as a tiki hut, a saloon, a 1960s den, and a park. "It felt a bit like being a student again," said Pete Docter.[2]

Over the next few years, the company expanded to occupy multiple buildings, including an office park across the street from the main office complex. After the success of *Toy Story* in 1995, Pixar purchased a new sixteen-acre lot in Emeryville, fifteen minutes south of Point Richmond near Berkeley. They planned their new building with two goals in mind. They wanted to renew the sense of community that had been lost as a result of their piecemeal earlier expansion. They also wanted to sustain and foster the old culture of spontaneity, fun, and creativity of Point Richmond.

To encourage unplanned collaboration and give employees opportunities to mix, they built an atrium at the centre of the building where everything that takes people out of their offices over the course of a day was located: entrance doors, the main stairwell, a cafe, conference rooms, screening rooms, and bathrooms. Pixar moved into the new building in 2000, during the final stages of work on *Monsters, Inc.* After initially feeling "that the place wasn't us," as Lee Unkrich said, "that it was somehow too nice for us," they began to quickly make the office their own. As Ed Catmull said, "You can feel the energy when you walk in the front door."

KEY TO PLATE

1: *Entrance gate*
Like the main buildings on Pixar's campus, the steel-and-masonry entrance gate is designed to pay homage to Emeryville's industrial past.

2: *Main Atrium*
The main atrium of Pixar's main studio building in Emeryville is their "town square" where employees from across the business can meet and interact throughout the day.

1

2

1

1: ***Iconic lamps***

The two-minute short film *Luxo Jr.* revolves around the relationship between a large "parent" desk lamp and a smaller, playful lamp, Luxo Jr. The writer and director of the film, John Lasseter, created this image with a marker pen on a slide.

SECTION 2

EARLY ENDEAVOURS

Even before its first feature film, Pixar's forays into computer animation turned heads and won awards. The hopping lamp from their first short became the studio's mascot and still lights the way today.

LUXO JR.

In the animated sequence at the start of every Pixar film, a hopping lamp squashes the letter 'I' in the word "Pixar". This lamp is Luxo Jr. and it was featured in the newly-independent studio's first short animated film.

At the time of the creation of that short, Pixar had forty employees. The company's main business was selling computer hardware, but Ed Catmull thought it would impress clients to create a short animated film to show what the computer could do. John Lasseter had been trying to learn modelling, so he was working on a digital model of a lamp that sat on his desk. When Catmull asked him to create the animated short, Lasseter decided to use the lamp. He showed work in progress at an animation festival, where it was pointed out to him by filmmaker Raoul Servais that, even though it was short, the film needed a beginning, middle, and end.[3]

A visit from a colleague's young son allowed Lasseter to observe the child's movements and proportions. He started to think about how baby proportions differ from adult proportions and he wondered what a young lamp would look like. He put his observations into his lamp designs. Working odd hours due to limited computer time, Lasseter began furiously animating this young lamp, mainly at night and sleeping on a futon under his desk.

The final short film is a masterpiece of simplicity in which a small lamp, Luxo Jr., plays with a ball – chasing it, balancing on it, jumping on it, and eventually deflating it – while a larger lamp, Luxo, watches on. The set is the surface of a plain wooden table and a black background. This avoided the expense of animating a fully realised background, but it also put the focus on the characters and the impressive use of light and shadows.

When Luxo Jr. was screened in 1986 at SIGGRAPH, it received a standing ovation. It became the first 3D computer-animated film ever to be nominated for an Academy Award.

KEY TO PLATE

1: Concept pastel
John Lasseter created this pastel drawing of the Luxo lamp.

2: Luxo wireframe
The "skeleton" that lies beneath the finished surfaces of the animation can be seen in this digital wireframe model of the Luxo lamp.

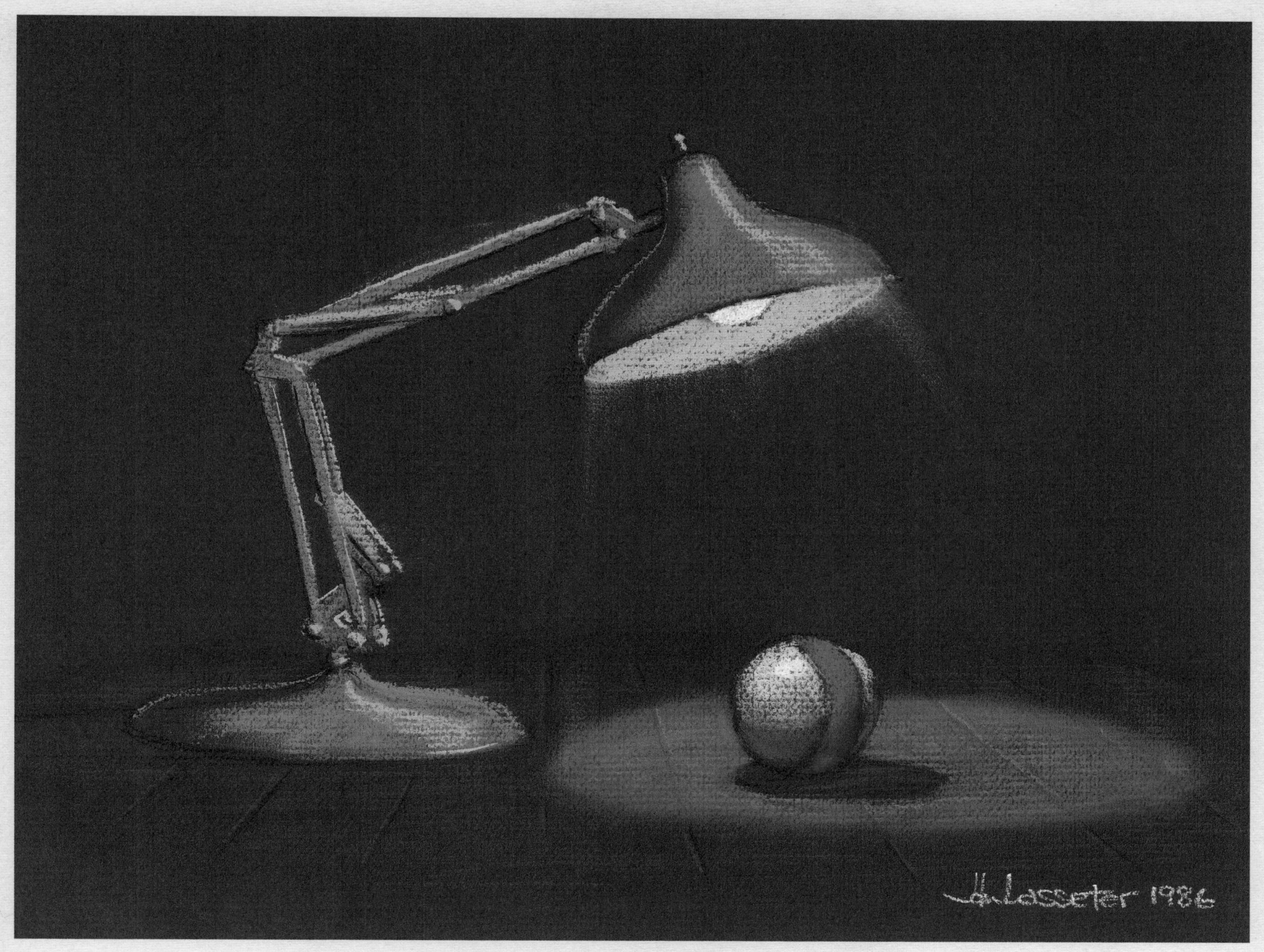
John Lasseter 1986

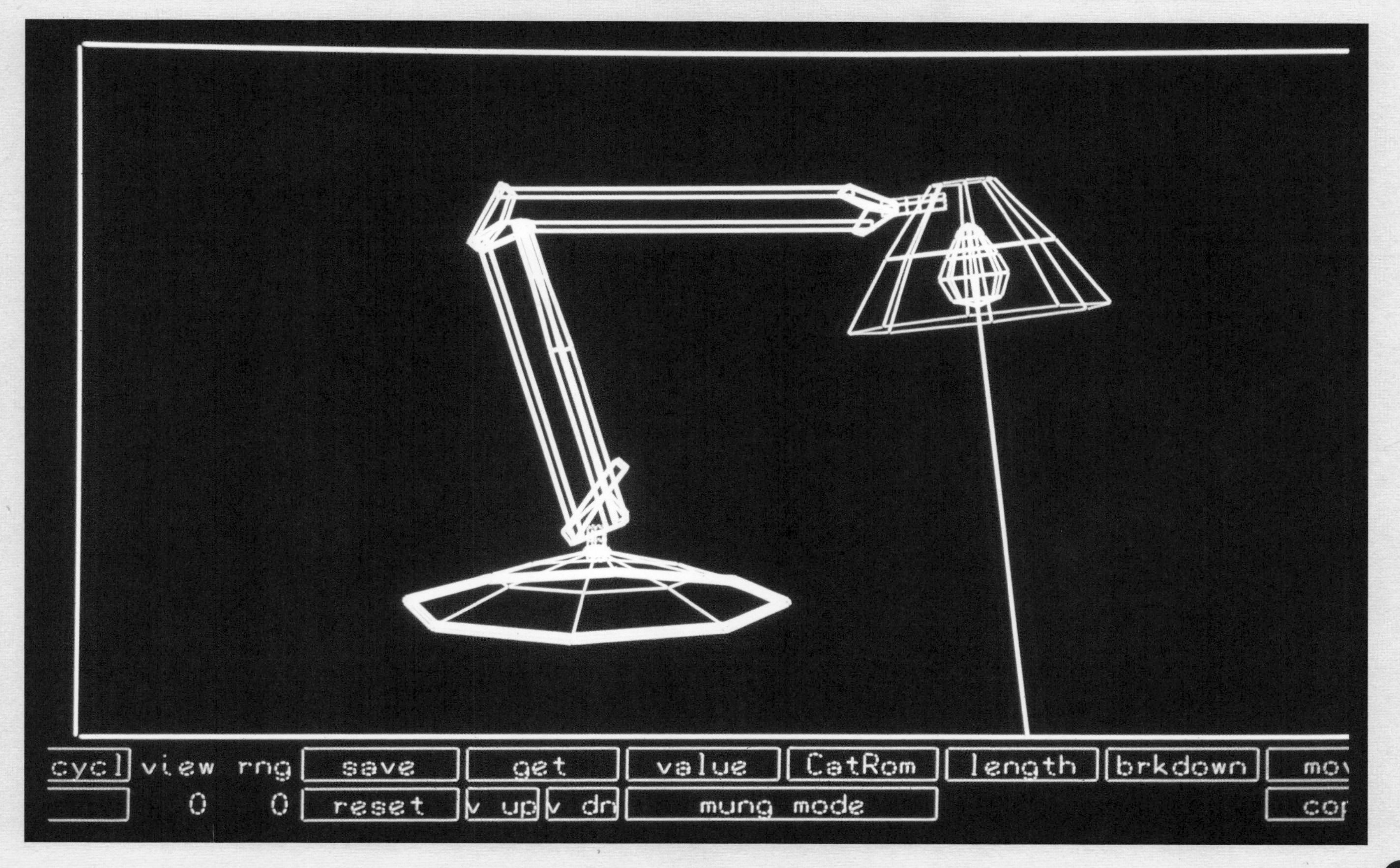
cycl
view
rng
save
get
value
CatRom
length
brkdown
0
0
reset
v up
v dn
mung mode

2

TIN TOY

Tin Toy, released in 1988, was Pixar's most ambitious short film to date. It had a longer and more complex story than previous short films, and complicated characters: a human baby and a wind-up, one-man band toy called Tinny with lots of moving parts. The film imagines what it would be like to be a toy in the hands of a baby. It was inspired by a home video of John Lasseter's infant nephew playing with his toys and putting each one in his mouth. At first the baby seems like a monster, and Tinny escapes under the couch, where he finds all of the other frightened toys. The twist comes when the baby hits his head and cries: Tinny bravely goes back out to help.

The five-minute film was first screened at SIGGRAPH in 1988 and it went on to win Pixar's first Academy Award: Best Animated Short Film. Significantly for Pixar, *Tin Toy* also caught the attention of the Walt Disney Company and discussions began for Pixar's first full-length feature, *Toy Story*, which was directly inspired by this ground-breaking short film. The deal with Disney would be signed in 1991.

The software used to create this short, as well as the other Pixar shorts, was developed in collaboration with Lasseter. By getting his feedback as the films were being made, the computer scientists were able to make the software much more user-friendly. One crucial change was that they now had separate tools for each stage of animation, which would allow several animators to work on different parts of a film at the same time. This would have huge significance when Pixar began to create their first feature-length animation. As Lasseter said, "The art challenges the technology, and the technology inspires the art."[4]

KEY TO PLATE

1: ***Storyboard***
This storyboard, drawn by John Lasseter, sketches out *Tin Toy*'s opening sequence, where the baby first appears.

2 and 3: ***Tinny's emotions***
In *Tin Toy*, the main character Tinny goes through a range of emotions on meeting a real-life baby for the first time. His initial delight quickly turns to fear and disgust as he sees how clumsy a baby can be!

1

2

3

1

1: ***Sweethearts***

Sheriff Woody has always had a soft spot for porcelain shepherdess Bo Peep in the *Toy Story* films. Digital artwork by Michael Yates.

SECTION 3

THE TOYS THAT STARTED IT ALL

Pixar's first feature-length film, *Toy Story*, was the first feature film to be computer-animated. Its unprecedented success put Pixar firmly on the map, spawning a beloved franchise and a cast of unforgettable characters.

TOY STORY
UNLIKELY FRIENDSHIP
ANDY'S TOYS
THE TOYS ARE BACK

TOY STORY

Work on Pixar's first feature film began in 1991, and the result, *Toy Story,* was released in November 1995. John Lasseter was already working closely with Andrew Stanton and Pete Docter when he asked them to help him to develop a story for an animated feature. They had mainly been working on the TV commercials that paid Pixar's bills. Stanton confirmed, "A large portion of us had never worked on a movie at all."[5] Joe Ranft had worked on films at Disney, such as *The Lion King* and *Beauty and the Beast*, and he and Lasseter had been talking about working together. In fact, the idea of doing more with the world of *Tin Toy* was one of Ranft's ideas, and he joined Pixar to work on *Toy Story* once the film was a go.

The story they started with was an adaptation of the unfinished *Tin Toy* Christmas TV special, with one-man band toy Tinny as the hero. But soon a new idea emerged: to contrast a new toy with a child's favourite old toy. They wanted to make a "buddy picture" where two conflicting characters would be forced to put aside their differences and work together. Eventually Buzz Lightyear replaced Tinny, and Woody became a cowboy – he had originally been a ventriloquist doll.

Several years into the process, in 1993, Pixar organised a work-in-progress screening for Disney executives. It wasn't a success; watching the reels with an objective eye, the Pixar team realised that they had lost sight of the story. Faced with the possibility that Disney would take the film away from them to finish it, Pixar made a huge gamble. "Just give us two weeks," Lasseter told Disney. Joe Ranft said, "I think that's where Andrew, John, Pete, and I really bonded as a group. It was do or die time."

The team worked day and night coming up with a new take on the story, completely remaking the first third of the film. The gamble paid off. Disney executives approved the sequences and the Pixar team could continue. Even so, getting to the finish line was hard for many reasons. They had never before completed a project of this scope and scale, nor in this medium. But at least now they were making the film they wanted to make. "To this day, *Toy Story* is the hardest, most exhausting, and still the most fun thing I've ever done at Pixar,"[6] said Bill Reeves, the film's supervising technical director.

When *Toy Story* was released, the response exceeded anyone's expectations. It was the best reviewed and top grossing film of the year. At the Academy Awards, Lasseter received a Special Achievement Award and the film's screenplay and score were nominated.

KEY TO PLATE

1: "Colorscript"
Art director Ralph Eggleston's pastel colour script for *Toy Story* was a tool that conveyed the desired feeling for the film – expressed through colour and lighting – which the digital artist then used to communicate the mood of each sequence. This "colorscript" was created in about a week.

1

UNLIKELY FRIENDSHIP

At the heart of *Toy Story* is the relationship between two toys. Woody, the favourite toy, is upstaged by the new arrival, Buzz Lightyear. Woody is a traditional cowboy doll with a pull-string voice box, while Buzz is a contemporary, shiny, new Space Ranger toy with lights and a range of phrases, including the now iconic line, "To infinity and beyond!"

Buzz Lightyear was originally named Lunar Larry and then, for a short while, Tempus from Morph. Woody, meanwhile, morphed from a ventriloquist doll into a loose-limbed cowboy doll, which helped reduce the scale differences between him and Buzz. The two characters were complete opposites from two different worlds – yet in their own ways, both were American icons, explorers of new frontiers.

Early in character development, Woody's character was not immediately likeable. In fact, he was mean-spirited and selfish, the idea being that he would become likeable over the course of the film. At that time, Tom Hanks came in to record his voice and commented, "This guy's really a jerk." The team ultimately made Woody more sympathetic – although, as top toy, he is still a bit selfish without realising it.[7]

Buzz was written to be aware of his status as star of a TV show, but when Tim Allen read the lines, a more no-nonsense, everyday attitude came through. The team realised there would be more comic potential and pathos if Buzz was not aware that he was a toy, but if he really did think he was a Space Ranger on an important mission.

KEY TO PLATE

1: ***Friends until the end***
The relationship between Woody and Buzz gets off to a rocky start before growing into a deep friendship, as seen in this digital artwork for *Toy Story 3*. Digital art by Robert Kondo.

2: ***Buzz Lightyear***
An early concept art version of Buzz Lightyear by Bud Luckey. His space ranger costume has red and yellow highlights here, instead of the blue and green shades that he ended up with.

In 2015, for the twentieth anniversary of *Toy Story*, this image was turned into a collectible metal pin.

1

2

ANDY'S TOYS

Toy Story had a strong supporting cast, allowing the filmmakers to indulge their love of toys of different types and eras. They studied each toy carefully, looking at how it was manufactured and whether it was cheap or expensive, before combining these factors to draw out each toy's personality.

Mr Potato Head, voiced by Don Rickles, is irritable and grumpy, as you would expect from a toy whose facial features are easily pulled off. Slinky Dog has a southern hound dog personality. His mix of growl and speech was inspired by Jim Varney's own dog, who sometimes seemed to be trying to speak. Hamm, the piggy bank, played by John Ratzenberger, is a know-it-all. He likes to sit on a high shelf and survey the goings on outside or inside the room. Bo Peep, voiced by Annie Potts, is a porcelain lamp who has a sweet friendship with Woody. Rex the dinosaur is played by Wallace Shawn. Despite looking big and ferocious, he is actually neurotic and insecure.

For the green army men, the animators made sure that they were as true to life as possible, down to the bent gun barrels, the bits of extra plastic around their heads from the moulding process, and feet that were attached to their bases. To study how they would move on their bases, Pete Docter nailed some shoes to a board and the animators hopped around the office wearing them.

KEY TO PLATE

1: ***Hamm***
As a money bank, Hamm is not technically a toy. Although, as this concept art shows, the animators gave him toy-like movements and a character to match. Pencil drawing by Ralph Eggleston.

2: ***Bo Peep***
Kind-hearted Bo Peep is the guardian of her three-headed sheep and she occupies the role of the voice of reason for all the toys. Disappearing before the events of *Toy Story 3*, she reappears in *Toy Story 4* as a much-changed character. Digital painting by John Lee.

3: ***Andy with his toys***
A colour script is created to establish the colour and the mood of each film. "Andy's room was home," reckoned lighting art director Dice Tsutsumi, who created this piece of digital art. "You knew what it was supposed to feel and look like."

4: ***Woody***
Woody was an edgier, more aggressive character at first, before the creative team rethought his personality. Pencil concept drawing by Bud Luckey, colour by Ralph Eggleston.

1

2

3

4

THE TOYS ARE BACK

The success of *Toy Story* quickly led to plans for a sequel, and the filmmakers already had a good idea. If *Toy Story* showed the heaven and hell of toys, with Andy's and Sid's rooms, what would purgatory be like? Being kept in the original box and owned by a toy collector, they decided.[8]

Toy Story 2 was originally planned as a modest direct-to-television sequel. However, John Lasseter persuaded Disney that the film deserved to be shown on the big screen. After the team at Pixar finished making *A Bug's Life*, which hit cinemas in 1998, the core creative team turned their attention to *Toy Story 2*, which would release in 1999. The film that had been developed so far was not up to par and needed to be revamped, with a release date just nine months away. "On paper, it wasn't possible to remake the film," said Ed Catmull, "but we did." The core team added many inspired new ideas, including Jessie's heart-wrenching song about kids outgrowing their toys. In the end, Pixar pulled off the impossible and the film became an even bigger hit than *Toy Story*.

1

Toy Story 3, released in 2010, was to be the final instalment, where a grown-up Andy was ready to give away his toys. The story group added a day care, as well as a new character created much earlier for *Tin Toy Christmas*: Lots-o'-Huggin' Bear. Lotso has become cynical about the toy-child relationship and tries to get Woody to see the world as he does. Animation techniques had advanced so much by the time *Toy Story 3* was made that the filmmakers knew they had to preserve the style of the earlier films while still taking advantage of technical advances. Believability, not realism, continued to be their mantra. The film won an Academy Award for Best Animated Feature. It was nominated for four others, including Best Picture.

Though Pixar had ended Andy's story arc, Josh Cooley remarked, "That's not the end of Woody's story." *Toy Story 4* released in 2019 and was about second chances, as Woody tackles the challenges of being with a new child, Bonnie. He meets Forky, made from bits of rubbish, and his old flame Bo Peep, who is now worldly wise and no longer loyal to just one child. Directed by Cooley, *Toy Story 4* was another critical hit, exceeding box office records for the previous three films and winning the Academy Award for Best Animated Feature. It was official: Pixar had broken every rule for sequels.

2

KEY TO PLATE

1: Collector's room
Woody in Al's display room, where toys were safe from being broken or chewed – yet destined never to be played with. Oil on paper and board by Randy Berrett.

2: Woody and Bo
Bringing porcelain shepherdess Bo Peep to life in *Toy Story 4* was a challenge for the animators. They began by studying in minute detail the glazing and cracking on porcelain, but, as noted by directing animator Patty Kihm, "If we had played her true porcelain, she wouldn't have moved at all." So they decided to break the truth to give her athletic movement. Digital painting by John Lee.

1

1: *Joy and Sadness*

Joy at the control panel inside Riley's head, with Sadness crouching in the shadows behind her. Digital painting by Ralph Eggleston.

SECTION 4

EXTRAORDINARY WORLDS

Pixar artists have brought some truly extraordinary settings to the screen, from the city where monsters live and a futuristic image of planet Earth, to a world inside the human brain and and a spirit realm beyond life and death.

MONSTERS, INC.

Pixar's fourth film, *Monsters, Inc.*, released in 2001. It began as a story about a man whose childhood drawings of monsters come to life. This was the brainchild of Pete Docter, who was Supervising Animator on *Toy Story* and was now directing his own movie for the first time. The story transformed into a focus on real monsters living in a world on the other side of bedroom closet doors. As Lasseter described it, "What if kids are telling the truth and there really are monsters in their closets?"[9]

With *Toy Story* and *A Bug's Life*, the filmmakers had been able to base their designs on real things, but since monsters were imaginary, the possibilities were endless. To help them get a handle on the look of the world, they commissioned some of their favourite illustrators to produce inspirational art. Ultimately, they decided that monsters wouldn't want to scare each other, so they designed the monster version of a factory town, which they called Monstropolis. For the monsters themselves, they took inspiration from animals and combined this with kids' impressions of what they thought monsters should look like.

The main characters emerged over time: Sulley, Mike, and the child Boo. Sulley's long, fluid hair was a technical challenge; the animators wanted to avoid having to create each strand by hand. They invented new software to simulate hair as it is moved by external forces, such as wind. This was a great technical breakthrough – and it made computer graphics look cuddly for the first time.

For the follow-up to *Monsters, Inc.*, Pixar decided to make a prequel, telling the story of how Mike and Sulley had become friends. *Monsters University*, directed by Dan Scanlon and released in 2013, captured the spirit of university, focusing on what happens when we end up in a completely different place to the one we had imagined.[10] The film is set a decade before *Monsters, Inc.* and the filmmakers carefully reverse-engineered everything to subtly suggest it was the 1980s rather than the 1990s.

Both *Monsters, Inc.* and *Monsters University* were commercial successes, bringing to life a beloved cast of new characters. *Monsters, Inc.* won an Academy Award for Best Original Song for Randy Newman's "If I Didn't Have You."

KEY TO PLATE

1: Monstropolis neighbourhood
"We always knew we'd eventually be in a 3-D world," said production designer Harley Jessup, who created this marker and ink concept artwork for *Monsters Inc.* "But we started with a 2-D, graphic approach."

2: Factory rooftop
The backstory behind the *Monsters Inc.* factory was that the post-war baby boom caused an increase in children's screams, and the factory expanded. Business dropped off when exposure to media violence made kids jaded. Acrylic concept art by Harley Jessup.

3: College days
The artists for *Monsters University* created a world where everyday objects and spaces were designed for monsters of all shapes and sizes. The architecture was decorated with monster-like details. Gouache by Ricky Nierva and Dice Tsutumi.

1

2

3

WALL•E

"What if mankind were forced to evacuate Earth and someone forgot to turn off the last robot?" Joe Ranft proposed this idea for a film during a brainstorming lunch with fellow filmmakers John Lasseter, Pete Docter, and Andrew Stanton in 1994, as *Toy Story* was nearing completion. The ideas that came out of that lunch provided the Pixar team with four future movies: *A Bug's Life*, *Monsters, Inc.*, *Finding Nemo*, and *WALL•E*,[11] which was released in 2008.

"*WALL•E* was a 'Robinson Crusoe' robot that you liked before you even knew what he was about," says Stanton. "You knew he was the last robot on Earth, working by himself. You immediately liked him."

WALL•E was originally developed by Stanton and Docter as a story called *Trash Planet*. Stanton, who took the helm of the project after finishing *Finding Nemo*, was intrigued by the idea of a love story between two robots. "There's something endearing about a machine that falls for another kind of machine he's never seen before," he said. He knew his robot would form his conception of love from watching the musical *Hello, Dolly!* on an old VHS player. Then, Stanton found a key image to signal the emotional core of the story. "It was the plant," he said: a single green shoot that emerges through the piles of junk on Earth. The image represented hope for Earth's regeneration and the revival of the human spirit. Stanton's theme for the movie was "irrational love defies life's programming" and, as co-writer Jim Reardon notes, "*WALL•E* falls in love with EVE the moment he sees her."

Stanton felt that the film could be done with minimal dialogue. The robots speak only in electronic noises, created by sound designer Ben Burtt, luminary of the *Star Wars* films and creator of R2-D2's voice, among much else. Even so, Stanton wrote an entire screenplay with the real dialogue for the robots in square brackets, which Burtt and the animators used to guide them. The animators studied the silent-era films of Charlie Chaplin, Buster Keaton, and Harold Lloyd, watching a film a day for a year. "You walk away from that thinking, 'What can't you tell completely visually?'" said Stanton.[12]

The ground-breaking film won plaudits from critics and audiences on its release, winning the Academy Award for Best Animated Feature and four other nominations. In 2010, *Time* magazine named it one of the best films of the decade.

KEY TO PLATE

1: New life
Director Andrew Stanton called the depiction of a small plant struggling to grow out of the trash the "key image" in *WALL•E*. He used it to re-centre himself when he became "lost in story land". Digital lighting study by John Lee.

2: Junkyard Earth
The abandoned Earth scenes were designed as a ghost town, with piles of trash forming an apocalyptic landscape inspired by locations such as the abandoned Chernobyl. Digital art by Paul Topolos.

3: WALL•E and EVE
This sketch shows the stark difference between utility robot WALL•E and the much sleeker EVE. "I could never drop the idea that it should really be a love story," said Stanton. Digital art by Ralph Eggleston.

1

2

3

INSIDE OUT

Director Pete Docter had created Monstropolis in *Monsters, Inc.* and a house lifted by balloons in *Up*. Now, with co-director Ronnie del Carmen, he decided to go inside the human mind for *Inside Out,* which released in 2015. Specifically, into the mind of Riley, an eleven-year-old girl going through the trauma of being uprooted when her family moves from Minnesota to San Francisco. Docter was inspired by memories of his own family moving to Denmark when he was a child, and by his daughter, who had recently become an adolescent. He asked, "What's going on in her head?"[13]

To answer this, the filmmakers brought in scientists, neurologists, psychologists, and other experts to understand how the mind and emotions work and how they change during adolescence. "Some psychologists claim there are as many as 27 emotions," says Docter. "We ultimately landed on five." The emotions of joy, sadness, anger, fear, and disgust became key characters in the film.

Inside Out takes place in the mind, not the brain: Docter didn't want to show blood vessels or nerve cells. The filmmakers visualised abstract concepts like memories and the subconscious.[14] "The designs emerged slowly, vaporous at first, gaining form and solidity," said Docter. Headquarters is the control room in Riley's mind and it's where Joy and the other Emotions guide Riley through her day. The subconscious was visualised as a mysterious, dark land, and long-term memory storage looked like a jelly bean factory. Memories are visualised in the film as fragile glowing globes, and dreams are made at Dream Productions Studios, "styled like a giant soundstage with sets and props," said Docter.

Defining the look of the Emotions was "probably the hardest thing we've had to figure out," said character supervisor Sajan Skaria. "They're not little people," said Docter. "They're made of energy." The glow around Joy, with particles radiating and shooting off her skin, had never been achieved before, and this effect required new software to be built.

The filmmakers essentially created two worlds – the real world and a world of thoughts, emotions, and memories inside Riley's mind. "It was like making two films," said production designer Ralph Eggleston.

The film, which premiered at Cannes Film Festival in 2015, was a triumph, winning the Academy Award for Best Animated Feature and wowing audiences and critics, who responded to its inventiveness and heart.

KEY TO PLATE

1: Bing Bong
Bing Bong was one of several imaginary friends the filmmakers came up with for Riley; ultimately the others weren't useful to the storytelling and didn't make the final cut. Bing Bong, part pink elephant and part stripey cat, drives a cart with rainbow boosters. Digital painting by Ralph Eggleston.

2: Joy
In some of the early concept art, emotions could "paint" feelings with light-energy. Digital painting by Ralph Eggleston.

1

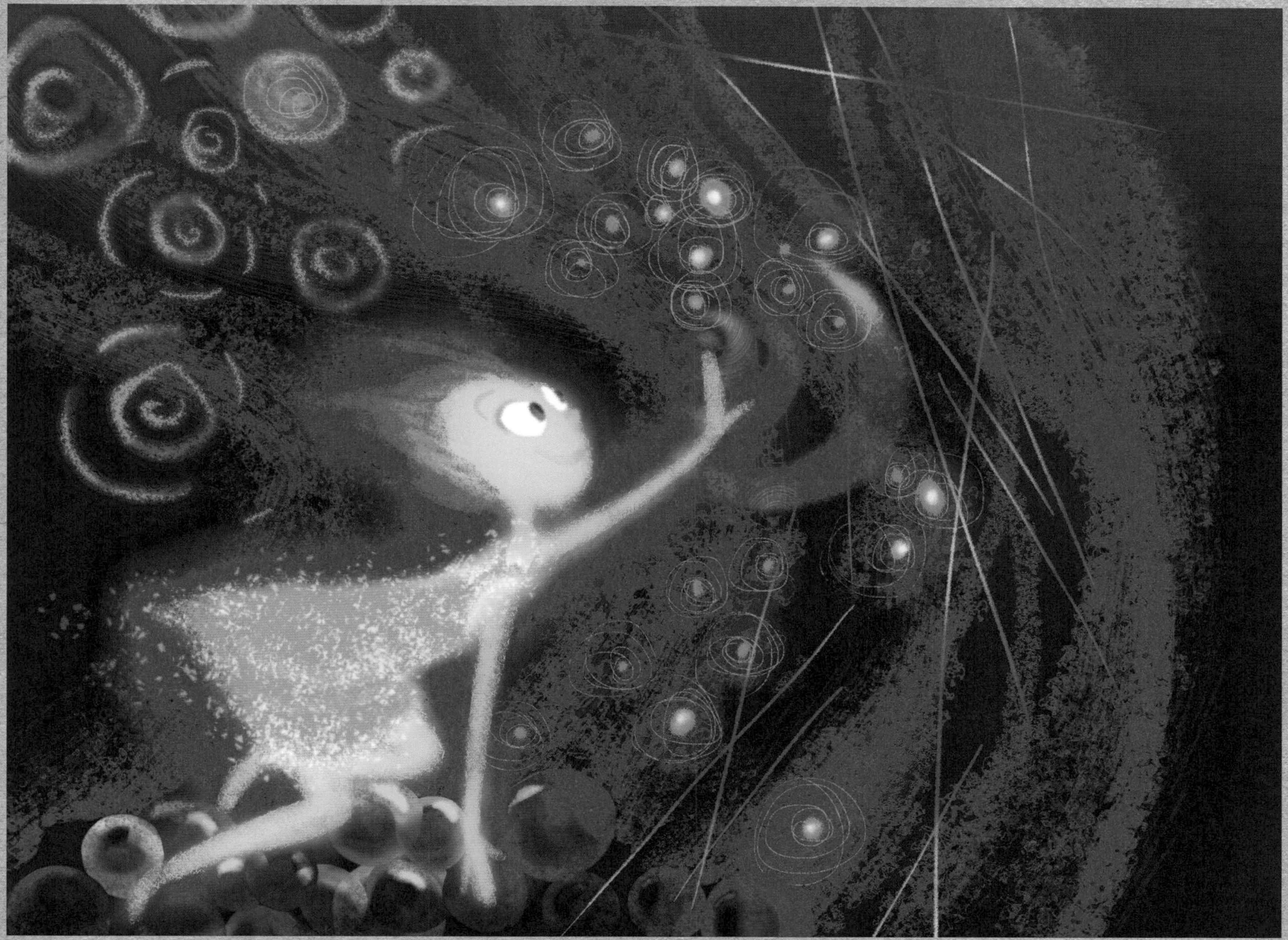

2

COCO

After directing *Toy Story 3*, Lee Unkrich pitched the idea of *Coco*, which centres around the Day of the Dead – the vibrant holiday celebrated in Mexico to honour those who have passed away. It would be Pixar's first film to feature a Latinx character in the lead role, and would release in 2017. For Unkrich, the film was rooted in a universal theme: the importance of family. He and co-director and writer Adrian Molina, producer Darla Anderson, production designer Harley Jessup, and other members of the team, made several trips to Mexico.[15] They witnessed how local families taught cultural practices to the next generation. They also collected the personal stories of Latinx team members and brought in Latinx cultural consultants to suggest ideas.

Coco is the story of 12-year-old Miguel Rivera who dreams of becoming a successful musician like his idol, Ernesto de la Cruz – a guitar hero and movie star inspired by stars of the golden age of Mexican cinema in the 1930s. Miguel's family has banned music, which leads to a momentous act of rebellion on Day of the Dead. This propels him into the glowing, colourful world of walking skeletons, winged spirits, and long-buried family secrets.

The filmmakers styled Miguel's village of Santa Cecilia – named by the filmmakers for the patron saint of music – with a sun-baked, daytime palette to contrast spectacularly with the vibrant, nocturnal explosion of colour in the Land of the Dead. The film also includes influences from everyday life in Mexico, including a floppy-tongued Xolo – the national dog of Mexico – as Miguel's loyal friend, and a two-dimensional prologue animated to look like *papel picado*, which is traditional tissue-paper art. Throughout the film, several main characters, voiced by a nearly all-Latinx cast, slip in and out of untranslated Spanish.

The film opened in Mexico on 20 October 2017, during the Morelia International Film Festival, the week before Day of the Dead. It became the highest-grossing animated film in Mexico's history. In the US, it released on 22 November 2017. The film won two Academy Awards, for Best Animated Feature and Best Original Song for Kristen Anderson-Lopez and Robert Lopez's "Remember Me."

KEY TO PLATE

1: *Vibrant backdrop*
"The bold and expressive sense of colour in Mexico is really unique," observed production designer Harley Jessup. Digital painting of a backdrop for a performance by Ernesto de la Cruz by Robert Kondo.

2: *La ofrenda*
Miguel at the *ofrenda*, or altar, where his family remembers their loved ones. Objects, such as food or photographs, are placed on the *ofrenda* to evoke the memory of the deceased. Digital art by Shelley Wan.

3: *Dreamer*
Miguel staring at the stars. "We all stand on the shoulders of those who came before us," says Director Lee Unkrich. Digital art by Ernesto Nemesio, layout by Robert Kondo.

1

2

3

SOUL

Two-time Academy-Award-winning director Pete Docter was already working on his new film, *Soul*, when he was promoted to the role of Pixar's Chief Operating Officer in 2018. Despite his new responsibilities, Docter elected to finish the film, which would release in 2020. It asks something all of us have wondered: "What makes you, you?" *Soul* follows Joe Gardner, a middle-school band teacher who gets the chance of a lifetime to play with jazz legend Dorothea Williams. But one small misstep takes him from the streets of New York City to The Great Before – a fantastical place where new souls get their personalities, quirks, and interests before they go to Earth. Producer Dana Murray said, "Like *Inside Out*, we're taking you to a world where no one's ever been – well, for a long time." Yet, as writer and co-director Kemp Powers said, "We went in a completely different direction than any of the other films that Pete's done."[16]

In the You Seminar, Joe meets 22, a soul who has never understood the appeal of the human experience. According to Docter, she's the teenager with the attitude: "You know, it's all boring and dull. Who cares? It's all stupid." Tina Fey, who voices 22, contributed some of the writing for the character in the script. Joe and 22 eventually team up and try to get his soul back to his body on Earth, which involves a journey through cosmic realms.

Joe Gardner, voiced by Jamie Foxx, is the epitome of the idea of the obsessional artist, or anyone with a passion – and how that passion can be "detrimental to the rest of your life," Powers said. Docter said, "I've been doing animation for 30 years. I love it, I can't get enough of it, and then I also recognise this is not the end-all, be-all of everything." For Docter, *Soul* asks, "What are the things that, at the end of the day, are really going to be the important things that you look back on and go, 'I spent a worthy amount of my limited time on Earth worrying or focused on that'?"

Docter and the filmmaking team discussed the concept of souls with representatives from different religious and cultural traditions to help them to visualise this non-physical entity. Docter said, "We're used to toys, cars, things that are much more substantial and easily referenced. This was a huge challenge." The filmmakers wanted the soul world to offer explanations for why life is the way it is – "everything from why a person has a certain personality to the ongoing futility of your favourite sports team," said Powers. Docter believes they're approaching grand questions about our very existence in a relatable way.

KEY TO PLATE

1: ***You Seminar***
Joe attends a You Seminar, a preschool for souls before they go to Earth. The artists imagined an ethereal space that blended the astral plane with a college campus. The result looks soft and mysterious. Digital art by Steve Pilcher.

2: ***Joe at the jazz club***
The goal for the design of New York in *Soul* was to make it feel physical, gritty, and realistic in order to accentuate the differences between the city and the ethereal Soul World. Digital art by Harley Jessup.

3: ***Fingers and keys***
A group of Pixar artists visited various New York jazz clubs to sketch and draw players and to gain an understanding of the improvisational nature of jazz. This research fed into the tone and feel of the film. Digital art by Tim Evatt.

1

the half note
THE HALF NOTE
VILLAGE
CAFE
RARE BOOKS
NOW APPEARING
DOROTHEA WILLIAMS
WITH
CURLY SANTOS
MAY ASAGI &
JOE GARDNER

2

3

1: ***Magic-filled skies***

Ian and Barley, with half of their dad, share a moment experiencing the magic of the universe. Digital art by Kyle Macnaughton.

SECTION 5

AMAZING JOURNEYS

"You have to take risks in life to have an adventure," says the Manticore in *Onward*. Many Pixar films are quests, wherein a character must travel far from home in order to discover themselves – encountering fun and adventure along the way.

A BUG'S LIFE
FINDING NEMO
UP
THE GOOD DINOSAUR
ONWARD

A BUG'S LIFE

Even before the release of their first film, *Toy Story*, in 1995, Pixar's filmmakers had started work on their second, *A Bug's Life*, which would release in 1998. For inspiration, they took one of Aesop's fables, *The Ant and the Grasshopper*, in which a lazy grasshopper sings while an ant stores food for the winter. When winter comes, the grasshopper begs the ant for food, but the ant refuses. Pixar asks the question: what if the grasshopper just stole the ant's food?

A Bug's Life is set in an ant colony which is being terrorised each year into giving up half its food stores to bullying grasshoppers. It takes an outspoken misfit, Flik, to turn the tables. Flik bravely leaves the colony to search for help, but the down-at-the-heels circus performer insects he brings back to the island don't seem like the fierce warriors the downtrodden ant colony needs.

Aware of the challenge often presented by projects that follow hit debuts, the filmmakers not only believed they needed to make a movie that could stand alongside *Toy Story*, they wanted to make something even bigger. They filmed the movie in widescreen Cinemascope, which allowed a lot of room for detail in each frame, but of course also increased the animation workload. This gave them a cast of thousands and the feel of an epic.[17]

But first, the filmmakers went on a field trip immediately outside the front door of their office. They created a tiny, wheeled cart to carry a camera, called the "bugcam," that allowed them to film from just above the ground. This brought about a key insight: grass, leaves, and flowers appear semi-transparent from an ant's-eye view and they are constantly moving in the breeze. There was also the matter of crowd scenes. An ant colony required hundreds of background ants to be in shot at the same time, all moving realistically. Specialist software needed to be developed to achieve this. The ants themselves were simplified to enhance their appeal: rather than standing on six legs, they stood upright, with two legs and two arms.

Despite the large cast of characters, the complex, multi-threaded storyline, and the epic animation task, the film eventually came together. It had a soundtrack by Academy Award winner Randy Newman. When the film released in 1998, it delighted audiences and critics. "I think *A Bug's Life* is the most beautiful film we've made," said Pixar director Lee Unkrich. "It's gorgeous; it's like a painting come to life."[18]

KEY TO PLATE

1: ***Ant colony***
Concept art showing the ants storing food. Acrylic painting by Tia W. Kratter, with layout by Geefwee Boedoe.

2: ***Grasshopper attack***
Concept art in acrylic paint by Geefwee Boedoe, showing the ant colony fleeing from the attacking grasshoppers.

3: ***Leaf bridge***
This piece was one of the touchstone images in the planning of the film. It captures the grandeur of the insect world as seen from ground level and the translucency that allows the insects' silhouettes to be seen from the other side of a sunlit leaf. Acrylic art by Tia W. Kratter, layout by Bill Cone.

1

2

3

FINDING NEMO

Finding Nemo, which released in 2003, is the story of an overprotective clownfish, Marlin, who sets out to find his lost son, Nemo, and meets a forgetful blue tang named Dory along the way. It is written and directed by Andrew Stanton, who co-directed *A Bug's Life*, and either wrote or contributed to screenplays for all four previous Pixar animated features. The idea of an underwater film came about in 1993 when *Toy Story* was only just in production. Stanton had been inspired when looking at fish at an aquarium, and, later, by his overprotectiveness towards his own young son. He decided to do something he didn't think had been done before in animated films: to tell the story from the point of view of the parent.[19]

By now, Pixar's filmmakers were experienced at animating bipedal characters – toys, insects, and monsters – but fish were completely different. They looked at fish in aquariums, scuba dived around coral reefs, and hired a professor of animal physiology to give them advice. The animators gave the fish expressive faces, adding eyebrow movements to signify emotion and, of course, made them talk.

Animating the underwater world was a challenge, too. Their first attempts were unsatisfactory. It was only when they set out to replicate three short pieces of real underwater footage that they realised they could do it. In fact, they did it too well: they had to make it less realistic to create a make-believe world. "We'd always wanted to do a CG animated film that looked like it was made in 1940, the three-strip Technicolour films where there were soft edges to things and a very soft look," production designer Ralph Eggleston explained. "We're not trying to replicate reality. We study reality and then we caricature it."

The film spent three and a half years in production. It was only when Pixar screened the first audience previews that they could see clearly what they had done, and it was a triumph. The film was released in May, rather than the usual November slot. It was a huge summer hit. It became the second biggest movie of the year and won the Academy Award for Best Animated Feature.

In 2010, when *Finding Nemo* was being readied for re-release in 3D to celebrate its ten-year anniversary, Stanton was ready with a sequel idea for Pixar to develop. It was based on some lines from *Finding Nemo*, when Dory says, "I forget things almost instantly. It runs in my family – well, I mean, at least I think it does... Uh... hmm... where are they?"[20] *Finding Dory* is about the memory-challenged blue tang as she's reunited with her family. It was a box office success when released in 2016.

KEY TO PLATE

1: The drop off
The safety of the reef behind Dory, Nemo, and Marlin is contrasted with the wide, unknown ocean beyond, as captured in a digital painting by Tim Evatt for *Finding Dory*.

2: Ocean swirls
The lighting in *Finding Dory* communicates information such as location and time of day, but also accentuates emotional states, such as sadness, anxiety, or joy. Digital painting by Ralph Eggleston.

3: Jellyfish
Marlin and Dory encounter jellyfish-infested waters in *Finding Nemo*. The colour dynamic of the film moves from the light blue of the reef to the darker colours of the dangerous wide ocean, to the green waters of Sydney Harbour. Pastel drawing by Ralph Eggleston.

1

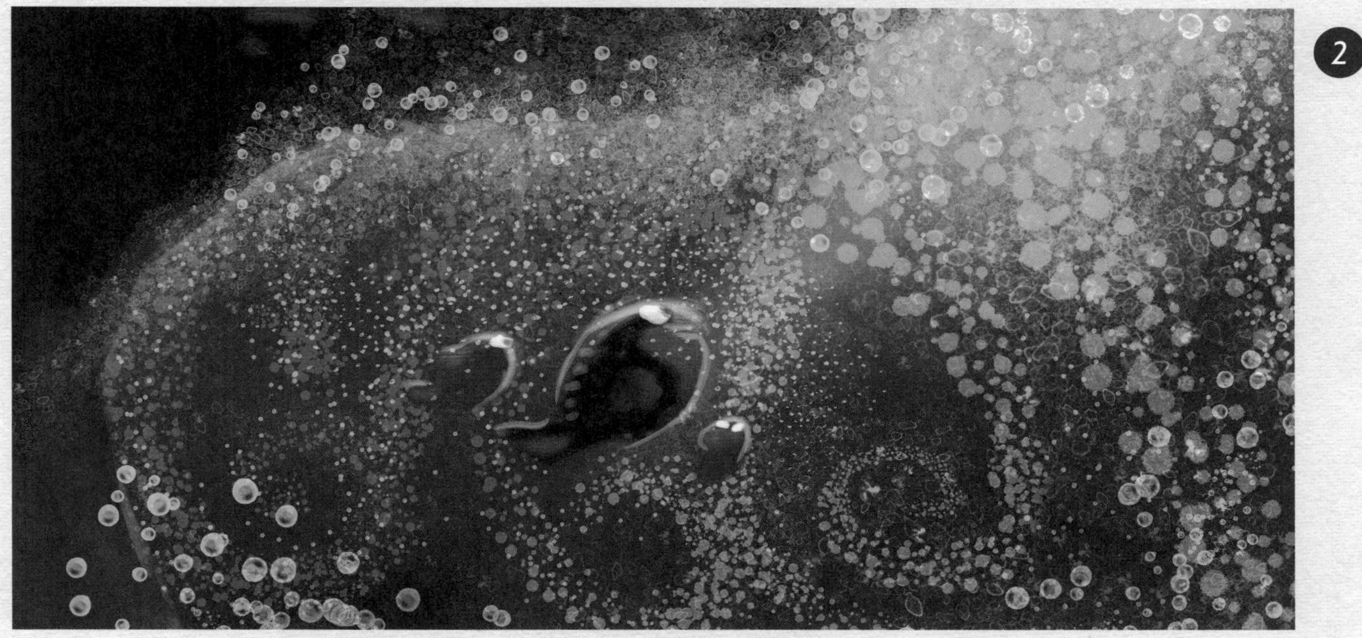

2

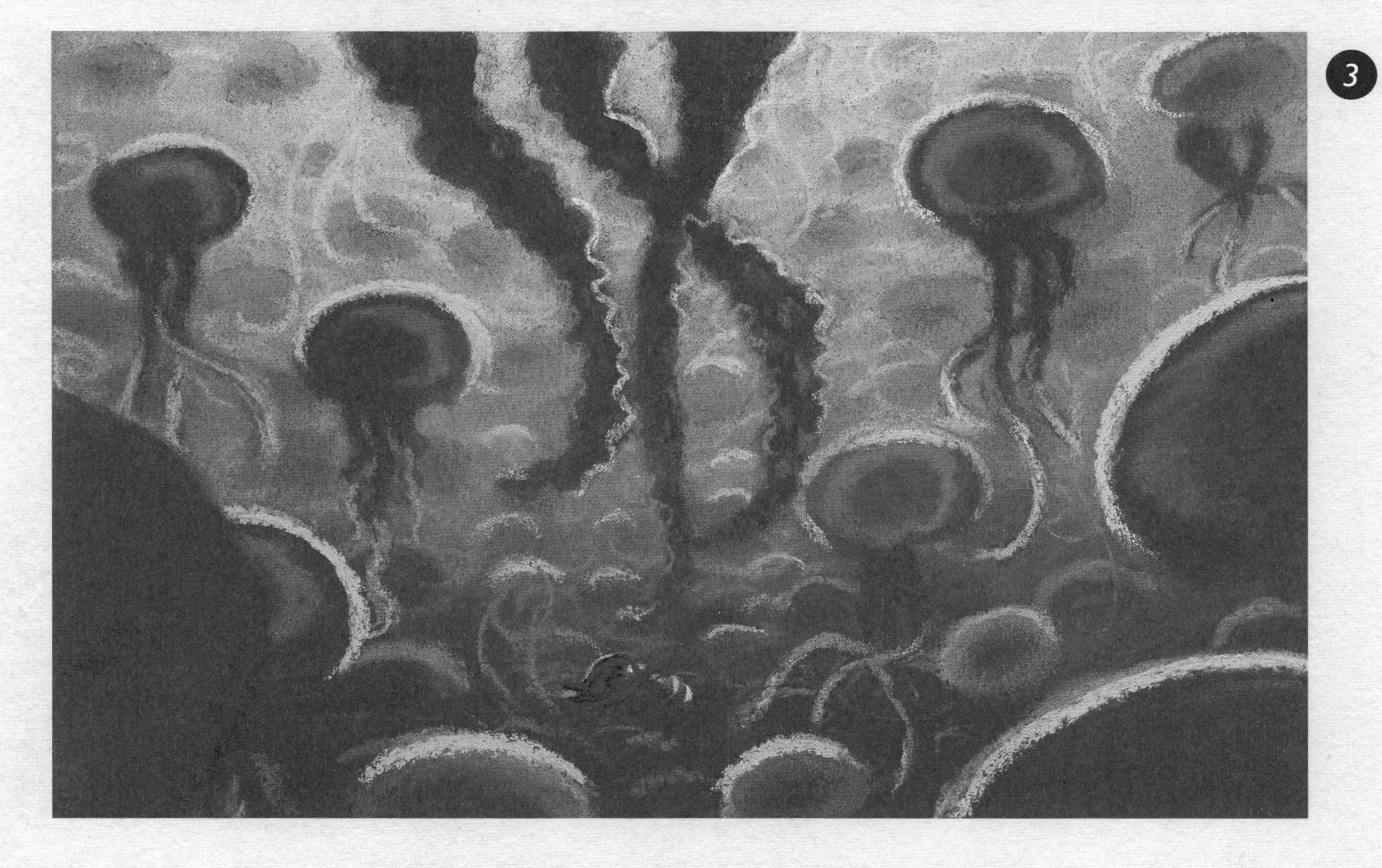

3

UP

Pete Docter said that his second film, *Up*, began with the thought of escape – something that he had often dreamed about.[21] After finishing *Monsters, Inc.*, he developed an idea about a floating city, which he and Bob Peterson – *Up*'s co-director and co-screenwriter – simplified into an idea about a flying house with just one occupant. *Up* released in 2009.

Docter had also sketched a humorous image of a "cranky old man selling the happiest balloons you'd ever seen." This became Carl Fredricksen, an elderly widower who had enjoyed a lifetime with his adventure-loving wife, Ellie. His one big regret was that they never realised their shared dream to visit Paradise Falls in South America. The film opens with a montage of scenes from their life together, which sets up the emotional heart of the movie. Carl is determined to honour his promise to Ellie and visit Paradise Falls, taking his house and thousands of balloons along with him. *Up* has been described by the filmmakers as an "unfinished love story" or a "coming of old age story."

Carl was voiced by legendary actor Ed Asner and based on the filmmakers' own grandparents, as well as actors such as Spencer Tracy or Walter Matthau. Docter said there was "something sweet about these grumpy old guys." The film's other lead character, eight-year-old Russell, was based on Peter Sohn, who went on to direct Pixar's *The Good Dinosaur*. Russell is missing an important person in his life, too: his father. When Russell comes into Carl's life, he brings a new energy that gives Carl permission to let go of the past and feel alive once again. "This is not just a comedy or a buddy picture," said Docter. "It's a love story."

The film's epic journey also takes in such colourful characters as a strange, giant bird that Russell calls Kevin, and a talking dog named Dug, to create a mesmerising, deeply affecting story. It was a critical smash and a box office hit, winning Academy Awards for Best Animated Feature and Best Original Score.

KEY TO PLATE

1: ***The Lost World***
For the parts of the film set in South America, the animators went on a field trip to research the alien-like landscape of tepuis, 1.5 km-high tabletop mountains in the rainforest. Gouache painting by Lou Romano.

2: ***Carl's house***
This piece captures the whimsy that the filmmakers wanted to achieve, which the film's producer Jonas Rivera called "a certain amount of 'once-upon-a-time' feeling." Gouache painting by Lou Romano.

1

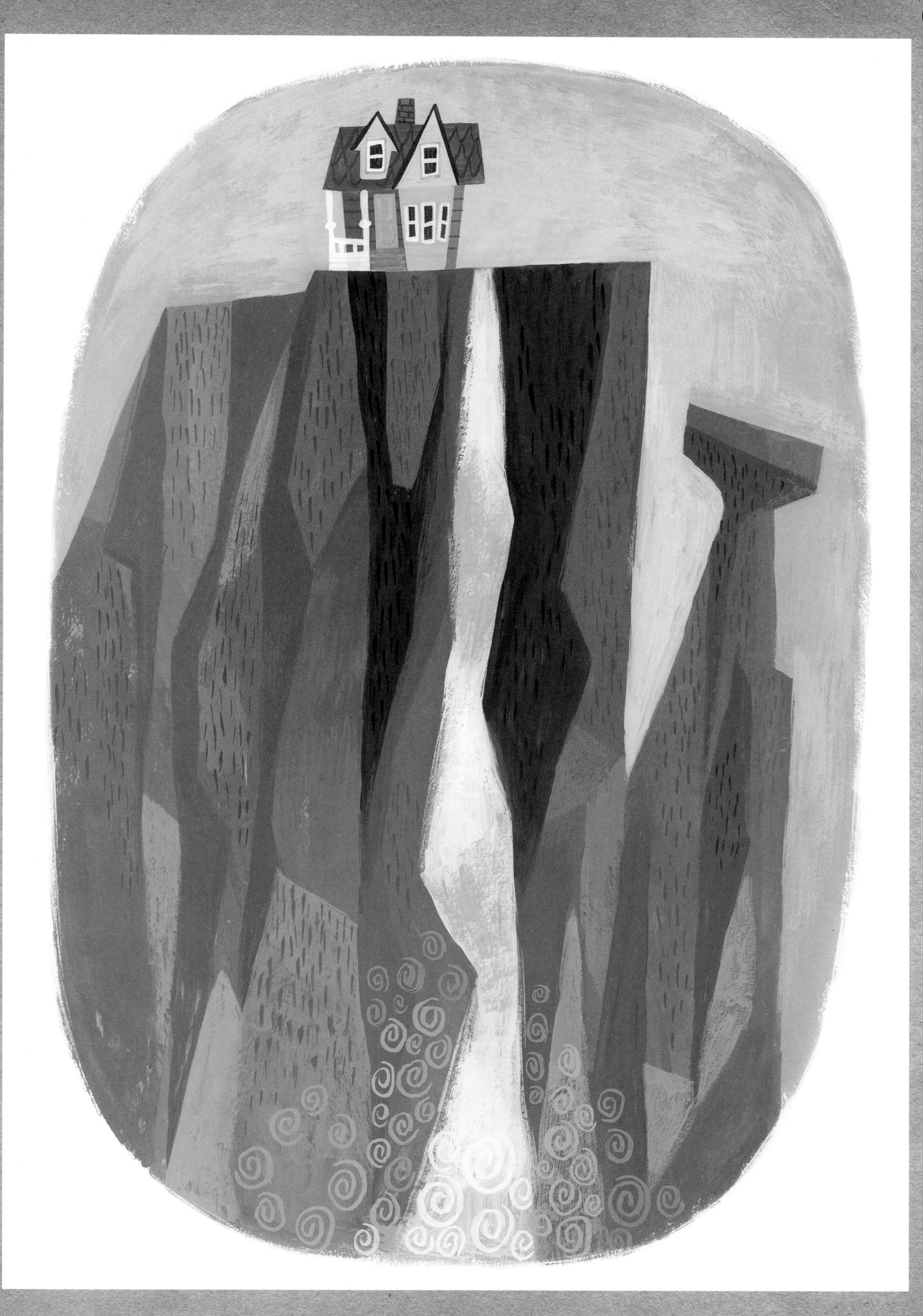

THE GOOD DINOSAUR

The Good Dinosaur was inspired by an idea that the co-director of *Up*, Bob Peterson, had in 2009: What if the asteroid that wiped out the dinosaurs 65 million years ago missed? Peterson, who remembered seeing animatronic dinosaurs as a boy at the World's Fair in New York, framed a story about a young Apatosaurus named Arlo who gets lost in the wilderness and makes friends with an adventurous human boy, Spot, who helps him overcome his fears. The film, which was released in 2015, became the feature directorial debut of Peter Sohn, who had directed the short film *Partly Cloudy* and had worked as a story artist on several Pixar films. One of the *Inside Out* co-writers, Meg LeFauve, wrote the screenplay. From early on, the filmmakers saw it as a classic boy and dog story. "Only in our story," Sohn said, "the boy is a dinosaur and the dog is a boy."[22]

The filmmakers made field trips to the rolling landscapes of Wyoming and Idaho in the northwest United States, where many dinosaur bones have been found. The team used US Geological Survey maps and satellite images from Google Earth to map out landscape features over huge distances, so the camera had the freedom to shoot in any direction. They also visited farming communities, which informed the idea of the plant-eating dinosaurs, such as Arlo, being farmers, and the meat-eaters, such as T. rex, being ranchers – which also gave the filmmakers an excuse to rewatch classic Western films for inspiration. Noting dangerous elements, such as landslides and quicksand, the filmmakers made the environment "the adversary for Arlo on his journey," according to set supervisor David Munier. Even storm clouds had an ominous, almost villainous presence, made more so by the fact that they were created for the first time as volumetric, 3D elements, rather than being painted onto the sets.

For Arlo, the filmmakers went to a zoo to observe the movements of elephants, which are large quadrupeds like dinosaurs. They even built a full-size model of the dinosaur from card and foamcore to get a sense of scale.

The finished film was shown exclusively prior to the US and UK premiere in 2015 at the gigantic Parisian cinema Le Grand Rex. *The Good Dinosaur* has a simplicity, with minimal dialogue and a focus on visual storytelling that belies the gargantuan effort of its creation.

KEY TO PLATE

1: Arlo falling into the river
Sohn wanted the river that Arlo follows to reflect his emotional journey: the waters are raging when Arlo is in turmoil and flow smoothly when he's finding inner peace. Concept art by Noah Klocek.

2: The wild west
Production designer Harley Jessup was inspired by classic Western movies, and Sohn wanted the dinosaurs to resemble cowboys – "Sam Elliot on horseback" noted animator Kevin O'Hara. Set design by Kristian Norelius and layout by Matt Aspbury.

3: Home on the range
After visiting Wyoming and Idaho, the filmmakers were inspired by "massive plains and plateaus, thundering rivers, and dramatic mountain ranges [that] would make even the largest dinosaur feel small", said director Peter Sohn. Lighting study by Sharon Calahan, layout by Erik Benson.

4: Arlo and Spot
A few lines capture the deep bond between central characters Arlo and Spot in this storyboard frame by Rosana Sullivan.

1
2
3
4

ONWARD

Dan Scanlon was a writer and director for *Monsters University*, a story artist for *Cars* and *Toy Story 3*, a member of the Pixar Senior Creative Team on *Brave* and *Inside Out*, and in 2017, it was announced that he would be directing a film set in a suburban fantasy world to release in 2020. Named *Onward*, the film's setting is one where magic has been replaced by modern conveniences, from mobile phones to fast food. All the magical races, such as elves and trolls, or "anything that would be on the side of a van in the seventies," Scanlon said, live in suburbia. Unicorns here are no longer majestic creatures, but now scavenge in bins for food. Scanlon explained that "this movie is a mixture of the fantastic and everyday."[23]

The film centres on two teenage elf brothers, Ian and Barley Lightfoot. Barley is older and more boisterous than his reserved younger brother Ian, and he is a big fan of quests – preferably hitting the road in his trusty, battered van, Guinevere.

When Ian turns sixteen, their mum gives them a staff and a magic phoenix gem – a gift from their father, who died shortly before Ian was born. The brothers have been given a magic spell that is able to bring their father back for 24 hours. However, the spell only half works – bringing back only the lower half of their father. With the gem destroyed, the brothers need to find another one before the twenty-four hours is up if they want to bring back the rest of him.

"At Pixar we try to create stories that come from some kind of personal truth," Scanlon said. "This film was inspired by my own relationship with my brother."[24] Scanlon was one year old and his brother was three when their father passed away. As teenagers, the Scanlan brothers heard an audio recording of their late father. "I have always wondered who my father was and that question became the blueprint for this movie," Scanlon said.[25] "My hope is some of the questions that I'm asking in the film will be questions other people are asking about their own lives."[26]

1

2

KEY TO PLATE

1: *Fairytale suburbia*
The artists wanted the neighbourhood in the film to be charming, but with a "sense of suburban normalcy," according to shading art director Bert Berry. So the fairytale mushroom houses come equipped with satellite dishes, the streets have power cables and lighting, and water towers dot the landscape. Digital art by Chris Sasaki.

2: *Elf siblings*
Brothers Ian and Barley Lightfoot were given distinct personalities. Barley is chaotic and idealistic, while Ian is more cautious. Digital art by Matt Nolte.

1

1: Legends

The classic racing cars in *Cars 3*, known as the Legends, were inspired by both vehicles and real-life personalities. The filmmakers undertook hours of research into the roots of stock-car racing and even spoke to some of the drivers. Digital concept art by Garrett Taylor.

SECTION 6

FOLLOWING A DREAM

Dreams in Pixar films come in all shapes and sizes – whether a rat aspires to become a chef, a sea monster wishes to experience life on land, or a princess doesn't want to marry the prince.

THE INCREDIBLES
CARS
RATATOUILLE
BRAVE
LUCA

THE INCREDIBLES

One of Pixar's goals was to always have fresh, exciting stories, and to make the studio a place where different voices could work together. Brad Bird had been an animation student at CalArts (California Institute of the Arts) with John Lasseter. Shortly after the release of Bird's animated debut, *The Iron Giant* (Warner Bros., 1999), Lasseter hired Bird. The seasoned director brought with him a new idea for a film – *The Incredibles*, which would release in 2004.

The Incredibles is about a family of superheroes forced to live ordinary lives after they are forbidden from using their superpowers. It was a film Bird had wanted to make for more than a decade. "I fell in love with it right away," said Lasseter.[27] The film is Bird's tribute to the pop mythology of his youth: spy movies, superhero comics, and his favourite TV shows. It takes place in a world that lovingly evokes a 1960s idea of the future. The film resonated on a personal level too, as Bird felt the pull of competing demands of family and work. He said he wanted to appreciate the "special gifts we are all given but don't always appreciate."

The film had a large cast of human characters – including three different body types for Mr Incredible alone.[28] "Creating a believable human being is pretty much the hardest thing you can do with a computer," said Lasseter. Pixar created a new muscle rig – a collection of synthetic muscles that move and change shape under animation controls – that allowed for realistic motion. A further huge advance in making humans look believable was a procedure called "subsurface scattering," which allowed light to penetrate skin surfaces and bounce back, creating realistic skin luminescence, as opposed to the flat, plastic look seen previously in computer-generated movies.

The Incredibles was the first Pixar film to win more than one Academy Award, including

1

Best Animated Feature and Best Sound Editing. It changed people's perceptions of what a Pixar film could be. It was a high-energy action-adventure and their first-ever PG rating.

Almost as soon as Bird finished the film, he had the core idea for a sequel – a role reversal between Mr and Mrs Incredible and an array of new powers for baby Jack-Jack. However, Bird worked on other films first, including *Ratatouille*, so it was another fourteen years before *Incredibles 2* was released to huge acclaim in 2018. It became Pixar's biggest-grossing movie to date and the third biggest animated movie of all time.

2

3

KEY TO PLATE

1: Mr Incredible
A striking poster representing the golden era of Supers, created for the wall of magazine covers and news clippings that Bob Parr keeps in his office. Digital art by Paul Rogers.

2: Title concept
The retro-futurist design of *The Incredibles* was expressed in this early titling concept by Teddy Newton. The story takes place in a futuristic version of the 1960s.

3: Elasticycle
Helen Parr, aka Elastigirl, on her Elasticyle, which was inspired by 1960s café racers – but with a futuristic transformation mode. Digital concept art by Ralph Eggleston.

CARS

Since *Toy Story*, John Lasseter had wanted to create a film about one of his life-long passions: cars. His dream turned into a reality when he took a two-month-long road trip across America with his family after finishing *Toy Story 2*. The trip brought clarity to the idea: a hotshot race car is forced to spend time in a small, forgotten town on Route 66, the iconic highway that had been superseded by the new interstate. *Cars*, which would release in the summer of 2006, would show the value in slowing down and learning that life is about the journey, not just the destination.

As ever, the production began with extensive research. The filmmakers went on field trips to speedways, stock car races, an auto show in Detroit, and to Route 66 itself. There they "found a grace and charm" to the towns that they "really fell in love with," said production manager Jonas Rivera.[29] They set out to capture all the telling details of these neglected towns – from peeling paintwork to tufts of grass between cracks in the concrete. Even though "you're just battling with the computer the whole way to make things less perfect," according to Lasseter. The film took six years to make, as Lasseter was juggling his job as director with his duties as Chief Creative Officer.

The film was a huge hit, nominated for an Academy Award, and it led to record-breaking merchandise sales. With further spin-offs in TV animation, theme park attractions, and a highly successful line of die-cast toys, *Cars* became a franchise on a grand scale.

On the worldwide publicity tour for *Cars*, Lasseter began to devise an idea for a sequel: an international race in which Lightning McQueen would be tested against the world's best race cars. When making a sequel, Pixar strives to do something distinctly different from the original film. *Cars 2*, released in 2011, is set in the glamorous world of Formula racing and involves a Hitchcock-type spy story, inspired by a discarded scene from the first film. Ten years later, Pixar returned to the world of cars once more. *Cars 3*, directed by Brian Fee and released in 2017, shows Lightning McQueen in danger of being made obsolete when he faces the next generation of race cars.

KEY TO PLATE

1: Hudson Hornet
In *Cars*, Doc Hudson aka 'The Fabulous Hudson Hornet' represented the link to an earlier age of dirt racing back in the 1950s. Pastel artwork by Bill Cone.

2: World Grand Prix
Cars 2 moves through four different countries. "It's more of a travelogue style," said director of photography-camera Jeremy Lasky. Digital concept art by Harley Jessup.

3: Thomasville Racetrack
The aesthetic of Doc Hudson's home track in *Cars 3* was inspired by abandoned dirt raceways encountered by the filmmakers in research trips around the back roads of North Carolina. Digital concept art by Garrett Taylor.

1

2

3

RATATOUILLE

Jan Pinkava dreamed up the inspired premise for Pixar's eighth film, *Ratatouille,* that would release in 2007. Pinkava, co-director of the film, had won an Academy Award in 1998 for Pixar's animated short *Geri's Game*. He explained that the film was about "a rat who wants to become a chef."[30]

The hero is a rat named Remy with sophisticated taste buds. The animators wanted him to be realistic as a rat, yet appealing enough for audiences to accept the idea of him cooking. Brad Bird, writer and director of the film, decided that the rats should walk on four feet and move like real rats. The animators worked with a rat expert and observed rat movements and behaviour close up. Remy, however, walks on two legs, showing that he's making a different choice in life. As a chef, he wants to keep his paws meticulously clean.

Bird was keen to ground the film in realism because the rest of the story was going to be wildly cartoonish. The lead human character, gangly Alfredo Linguini, displayed more physical slapstick than the studio's previous characters. As Pinkava said, "We wanted to give the characters and sets a puppet-y look – that feeling you get with scale figures, puppets, or stop-motion animations."

The film's setting, Paris, is lovingly recreated by the animators, who exaggerated the height of every window, the ornateness of the ironwork and the sag of the masonry, to

1

2

create a recognisable but caricatured City of Light. They brought a special believability to the restaurant kitchen, where much of the action was set. This was inspired by visits to the city's top restaurants and, back in California, chef Thomas Keller's French Laundry restaurant, which was designed in the French style. Keller also created the haute cuisine version of the ratatouille dish seen in the film.

Ratatouille was a critical and global box office success, winning the Academy Award for Best Animated Feature and nominated for four other awards, setting a new record at the time for the most nominations for a computer-animated film. It was especially well received in France, where it became the country's biggest ever animated film debut, and it inspired a theme park ride at Disneyland Paris.

3

4

KEY TO PLATE

1: Paris street
Production designer Harley Jessup said, "We styled and caricatured things to create a sort of fairy-tale Paris." Colour study by Harley Jessup, digital.

2: Restaurant kitchen
Remy peeks into the world he longs to experience: a professional kitchen in a world-class restaurant. Concept art in pastels by Dominique Louis, layout by Harley Jessup.

3: Remy's big break
Story supervisor Jason Katz said being in a professional kitchen is "like being backstage at a play, or at a rock concert. It just feels cool." Digital painting over set render by Dominique Louis, with character layout by Jason Deamer.

4: Paris rooftops
In a key moment in the film, Remy and Emile take in the view of Paris from above instead of from below, from where they usually see it. For Remy, in the words of Brad Bird, "everything suddenly opens up and [he] sees the vast, magical expanse of Paris." Pastel by Dominique Louis, layout by Harley Jessup.

BRAVE

Brave, released in 2012, was Pixar's first fairy tale and period film, set in medieval Scotland. It centres on Merida, a sixteen-year-old princess and skilled archer, who defies her parents' desire for her to marry and instead chooses her own path in life. Directed by Brenda Chapman, who also wrote the story, and Mark Andrews, the film was inspired by Chapman's relationship with her own daughter: "Our love and our battle of wills," she said. Chapman was also inspired by classic fairy tales, though she knew the film had to be unique: "There was no room for a prince or other love interest to come along and save the day," she said.[31]

The filmmaking team made two research trips to Scotland. They were impressed by the terrain and the people, but knew that the setting would present them with huge technical challenges. As John Lasseter said, "Medieval Scotland is as far from an environment that is natural for computer animation as you can possibly get. Forests, fields of grasses and heather, craggy rocks covered with lichens and mosses... even the man-made objects, hewn from rock and wood and hammered out of iron and steel, are irregular. The animals, from the king's dogs to Merida's horse, Angus, to the bears at the heart of the story are shaggy, furry, and muscled. Humans have freckles and wrinkles and layers of clothing, all of different weights and textures. And don't forget Merida's spectacular hair."

When the resulting film premiered in 2012 it won the Academy Award for Best Animated Feature. But the film also provided young girls with a strong role model in Merida, who, Chapman said, is "a great leader – in her own right, in her own way."

KEY TO PLATE

1: Castle DunBroch
One of Castle DunBroch's inspirations was a thirteenth-century castle that stands on the small island of Eilean Donan in the Scottish Highlands. The filmmakers also used the constantly changing and dramatic weather conditions they witnessed on their research trips in their storytelling. Digital art by Steve Pilcher.

2: Merida and the bear
Production designer Steve Pilcher's first acrylic painting for the film shows the dramatic scale relationship between Merida and her mother when she has transformed into a bear.

3: Merida
According to Steve Pilcher, who created this acrylic and digital artwork, "We really thought about how Merida's red hair would be accented in different environments."

4: Tapestry
According to producer Katherine Sarafian, "The tapestry design was set from the beginning [...] It's a great representation of all that's in the film." Digital artwork by Steve Pilcher.

1

2

3

4

LUCA

Pixar's twenty-fourth feature film, released in 2021, was a coming-of-age tale set in a sun-drenched seaside town on the Italian Riviera. It focuses on teenage friends Luca and Alberto, who, secretly, are sea creatures that appear human only on dry land. As their friendship develops over the summer, the boys enjoy themselves Italian-style, with gelato, pasta, and scooter rides, and they befriend a human girl along the way. "In addition to the beauty and charm of the Italian seaside," said director Enrico Casarosa, "our film will feature an unforgettable summer adventure that will fundamentally change Luca."[32]

The film was Casarosa's feature-length directorial debut after his Academy Award-nominated short film *La Luna*, which released with *Brave* in 2012. Prior to this, Casarosa worked as a storyboard artist on such films as *Ratatouille* and *Up*. Casarosa was himself born in Genoa in Italy and has spoken of how personal the film is to him: "My summers were spent on beaches. I met my best friend when I was eleven. I was really shy and I found this troublemaker of a kid who had a completely different life. I wanted to make a movie about those kinds of friendships that help you grow up."[33]

As well as owing a debt to the Disney classic *The Little Mermaid*, Casarosa was inspired by Italian filmmaker Frederico Fellini, whose films blend fantasy and realism, and Hayao Miyazaki, co-founder of Japan's Studio Ghibli and director of *Spirited Away*, *Howl's Moving Castle*, and many others. During the research phase of the film's development, the Pixar team visited Cinque Terre, a series of centuries-old villages in northwest Italy, with their cameras and sketchbooks. Character designer Deanna Marsigliese, herself of Italian parentage, said, "We were sent to Cinque Terre to explore and collect inspiration." Even though Marsigliese was familiar with her own "slice of Italy", she found that going back and observing with an eye for *Luca* was "really exciting".[34] Her designs for Luca as a sea monster, with green skin, large eyes, and gills, were inspired by the *Creature from the Black Lagoon*, with the unworldly but gentle charm of the amphibious man from *The Shape of Water*.

The premise may be fantastical and otherworldly, but, at its core, *Luca* is a story about love, friendship, and acceptance. "Childhood friendships often set the course of who we want to become," said Casarosa, "and it is those bonds that are at the heart of our story in *Luca*."

KEY TO PLATE

1: Luca in the attic
Sunlight filters in through the ceiling of the attic in this digital painting from the colour script by Daniel López Muñoz. "Joy, sadness, fear hope – the Meditterranean summer sun offered a unique and honest warmth and vitality of colour that is ultimately central to the themes we wanted to convey," noted Muñoz.

2: Luca in the water
Luca shows his human side above water and his sea creature self below the surface, in a pencil and digital painting by Daniel López Muñoz.

1

2

1: ***Voyage of discovery***
Pixar's Sparkshorts programme brings in new voices and approaches to animation. The nine-minute film *Loop* explores the need for connection between a non-verbal autistic teenage girl and a teenage boy who are on a canoe trip together. Digital painting by Paul Abadilla.

SECTION 7

SHORT FILMS AND THE SMALL SCREEN

From the beginning, Pixar artists have embraced the art of short films, sharing them on both the big and small screen. These mini masterpieces tell fully realised stories in a concise way.

TOY STORY AND CARS SHORTS
ORIGINAL PIXAR SHORTS
SPARKSHORTS
COMPANION STORIES

TOY STORY AND CARS SHORTS

In 2000, Pixar's characters moved into the world of television for the first time with the debut of *Buzz Lightyear of Star Command*. Pixar created the opening computer-animated sequence, while Disney Television Animation produced the bulk of the sixty-five-episode series using traditional 2D animation. The series aired on UPN and ABC, and was later released for home viewing.

After the success of *Cars* in 2008, Pixar began releasing a series of shorts under the umbrella title *Cars Toons*. The first series was called *Mater's Tall Tales*, featuring Lightning McQueen and the naive tow truck Mater. In each of the eleven shorts, Mater tells Lightning McQueen an unlikely but supposedly true story from his past. One of the shorts, *Tokyo Mater*, directed by John Lasseter and co-directed by Rob Gibbs and Victor Navone, released in cinemas in the US in front of Disney's *Bolt*. The second series was called *Tales from Radiator Springs*, featuring various characters from *Cars*. One of the four shorts is *Radiator Springs 500 ½*, directed by Rob Gibbs and Scott Morse in 2015. The other three, each at just over a minute in length, were referred to as "shorty shorts." They were shown on the Disney Channel from 2013 to 2014.

Beginning in 2011, Pixar released a group of shorts called *Toy Story Toons*, which are set after the events of *Toy Story 3*. The first, *Hawaiian Vacation*, directed by Gary Rydstrom, features Ken and Barbie going on a romantic holiday to Hawaii – actually faked by the rest of the toys in Bonnie's bedroom. It was shown with the theatrical release of *Cars 2* in 2011. In *Small Fry*, directed by Angus MacLane, Buzz Lightyear meets a smaller, meal toy version of himself. It was shown with the theatrical release of Disney's *The Muppets* in 2011. In *Partysaurus Rex*, directed by Mark Walsh, dinosaur Rex leads a rave in Bonnie's bathtub – with music created by electronic dance artist BT. It was released with the 3D theatrical re-release of *Finding Nemo* in 2012.

Forky Asks a Question is an animated streaming series where Forky, the lovable spork from *Toy Story 4*, asks other toys questions about concepts he doesn't understand, among them money, love, time, and cheese. Directed by Bob Peterson, eight episodes released in 2019 and two in 2020 on Disney+.

Between 2013 and 2014, Pixar released two television specials. The first, *Toy Story of Terror!*, written and directed by Angus MacLane, is a twenty-two-minute-long tale that was created for Halloween. It features the toys getting stranded at a roadside motel where eerie occurrences take place. The second, *Toy Story That Time Forgot*, was written and directed by Steve Purcell. Originally planned as a six-minute short, it was expanded to a twenty-minute holiday special, featuring dinosaurs Rex and Trixie.

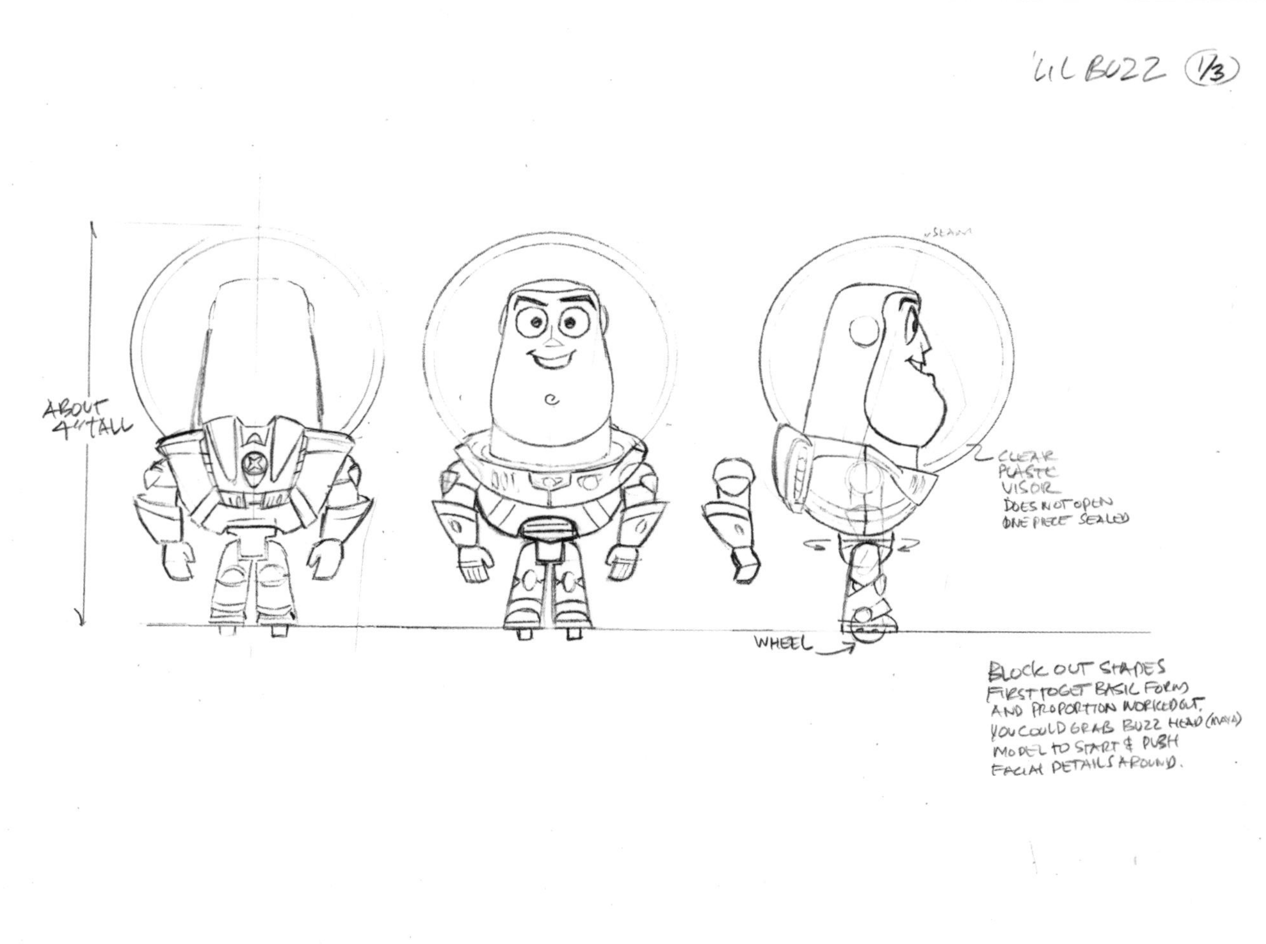

KEY TO PLATE

1: **Mater Private Eye**
This film noir-inspired *Mater's Tall Tales* episode told a tale of Mater as a private investigator. It was created all in black and white.

2: ***Poultry Palace Buzz***
For *Small Fry*, director Angus MacLane was inspired by his love of fast food toys: "There's something about fast food toys that feels really unloved," he said. Pencil art by Bob Pauley.

ORIGINAL PIXAR SHORTS

In the 1890s, when cinema was a new art form, all films were short. Peepshow-like devices called Kinetoscopes played short snippets of real life and current affairs to individual viewers. In the 1910s, the first purpose-built "picture palaces" showed longer feature films. These films were typically preceded by original short films, as well as newsreels and, sometimes, live acts. By the 1960s, trailers and commercials had mostly replaced short films. However, short films remain popular with visual artists, and Pixar has revived interest in them. Many Pixar films have been shown in cinemas with an original short film preceding them.

Pixar's early short films in the 1980s were both vehicles for storytelling and opportunities to show a new piece of software or a technique. Short films also enable filmmakers to develop their skills. "People do a wider range of work on a short," said Pixar's former President Ed Catmull, "so it is a better training ground than a feature film to get a broad view of production."

Short films took a backseat while Pixar focused on producing their first full-length feature, *Toy Story*. *Geri's Game*, shown with *A Bug's Life* in 1998, became the first of a second generation of Pixar shorts. Director Jan Pinkava was inspired by memories of his own chess-playing grandfather, who would at times play games against himself. The film pushed Pixar's abilities to create human characters and realistic clothing. It won an Academy Award for Best Animated Short Film.

Pixar's next short film, *For the Birds*, directed by Ralph Eggleston, also won an Academy Award. Premiered in 2000, then released with *Monsters, Inc.* in 2001, it tells the story of a variety of small birds and one large bird who aren't getting along. Their teasing and fighting leads to a surprising end. Many more Academy Award nominations would follow, with two further wins to date: *Piper* in 2016, about a baby sandpiper overcoming her fear of water, and in 2018, *Bao*, a story about a mother learning to allow her son to grow up. Pixar's short films have come to employ a wide array of styles, sometimes even using traditional 2D animation. "Short films are part of Pixar's DNA," said Lasseter. "It's where we started, and as we grew we knew we wanted it to be a part of Pixar going forward."

KEY TO PLATE

1: **Day & Night**
Shown before *Toy Story 3* in 2010, *Day & Night* is the story of two characters who learn to appreciate their differences. Unusually for Pixar, hand-drawn animation was used for the character outlines; only the scenes inside the silhouettes were created in 3D animation. Teddy Newton, digital.

2: **The Blue Umbrella**
German-born director Saschka Unseld's *The Blue Umbrella*, released in 2013, was inspired by finding an umbrella on the street in San Francisco. This love story between a red and a blue umbrella is told, like most Pixar shorts, without dialogue. Digital painting by Saschka Unseld.

3: ***Temple deity***
Sanjay's Super Team preceded *The Good Dinosaur* in 2015 and imagines Hindu gods as superheroes. Director Sanjay Patel was inspired by "how I grew up with my father and how we both had our respective forms of devotion and the culture clash it created." Digital art by Sanjay Patel.

1

2

3

SPARKSHORTS

SparkShorts is an experimental storytelling initiative at Pixar that encourages new creative voices at the studio to share their stories. A small team is given just six months and a limited budget to develop a short animated film. "The programme was created to provide opportunities to a wide array of artists – each with something unique to say," said Lindsey Collins, Vice President of Development for Pixar.[35] Jim Morris, President of Pixar Animation Studios, adds, "The SparkShorts programme is designed to discover new storytellers, explore new storytelling techniques and experiment with new production workflows. These films are unlike anything we've ever done at Pixar."

One SparkShort film, *Purl*, directed by Kristen Lester, features a brightly coloured ball of yarn named Purl who gets a job in an office dominated by men. Lester was inspired by her own early experiences in animation. She says, "I was often the only woman on the team I was working with. I just wanted to be one of the guys, so I could have friends and colleagues." At Pixar, however, she learnt "acceptance of myself, and the fact that I was a woman and I work in this business." This epiphany becomes the theme of *Purl*. It was released at SIGGRAPH in 2019, where it was named Best in Show, and then shown at El Capitan Theatre and on YouTube and Disney+.

Smash and Grab is a mini-action adventure about two robots making a daring escape from the engine room of a futuristic locomotive. Under director Brian Larsen, the team experimented with a new production process. For example, animators would wear motion-capture suits to translate real body movements directly into the computer: a new way to conceive of storyboarding and location scouting.

Moving in the opposite direction, *Kitbull*, written and directed by Rosana Sullivan, is all about drawing: unusually for Pixar, it is animated in a 2D style. Set in the Mission district of San Francisco, it follows an unlikely friendship between a stray kitten and an abused pit bull. In common with other SparkShorts, it shows a willingness to look at slightly more

1

2

3

4

5

6

mature themes than typical Pixar films, and it was nominated for an Academy Award.

Float is a short film directed and written by Bobby Rubio, who said that his autistic son inspired the story. In the film, the son has the ability to float. "Floating, to me, just visually looks beautiful," Rubio said. Producer Krissy Cababa observed, "It's the story of any child's difference, it doesn't necessarily have to be autism." For Rubio, the film becomes about accepting who his son is, not who he wants him to be.

Another highly personal story is told by director Edwin Chang in *Wind*. It was inspired by his grandmother, who fled the Korean War and brought up four boys, making every sacrifice to help them to settle in the US. In the film, the boy and his grandmother are trapped on a floating rock, symbolising "a broken place, a place of lost opportunity," according to Chang, they must build a rocket to escape.

Loop, directed by Erica Milsom, features a non-verbal, autistic girl and a talkative boy who must loop a lake on a canoe together. For Milsom, the film explores "that place between two people who don't share a common language. It's a language you have to feel out and find a means of communicating with each other that's very personal." These inspirational and diverse shorts are just the beginning – additional films in the SparkShorts programme are in production.

KEY TO PLATE

1: **Purl** ***poster***
The official poster depicts the moment when Purl first enters the fast-paced, high energy, male-centric office of B.R.O. Capital.

2: **Smash and Grab** ***poster***
The poster for *Smash and Grab*, a short about two robots who decide to make a break for freedom, reflects the film's distinctive Art Deco sci-fi design.

3: **Kitbull** ***poster***
Graffiti art and a scratchy hand-drawn aesthetic dominates the poster of *Kitbull*, reflecting the film's gritty urban setting.

4: **Float** ***poster***
The poster for *Float* focuses on the positivity and exuberance of Alex's special ability to float, the moment when his father is no longer ashamed of him for being able to do so.

5: **Wind** ***poster***
In the poster for *Wind*, Ellis, who is tethered to his grandmother, gazes towards the bright light at the top of the mysterious sinkhole in which they live.

5: **Loop** ***poster***
Renee and Marcus take an urban canoe trip, where they learn to communicate and understand each other, in the poster for *Loop*.

COMPANION STORIES

Pixar has extended the imaginative worlds of its films to additional short films that tell side-stories or further adventures.

Originally a scene in *The Incredibles*, the idea for the short *Jack-Jack Attack* was cut from the feature film and later expanded. Written and directed by Brad Bird, it's about Kari the babysitter as she looks after Jack-Jack while the rest of the superhero family are out saving the day. It premiered on the 2005 home entertainment release of *The Incredibles*, and was part of the Pixar Short Films Collection, Volume 1, a home video compilation.

BURN·E features a minor droid from *WALL·E* in a short adventure that takes place concurrently with the events of the film; moments from the main film are intercut into scenes in the short. Directed by Angus MacLane, who wrote it with *WALL·E* director Andrew Stanton and Derek Thompson, it was created at the same time as the film. It premiered on the 2008 home entertainment release of *WALL·E*, and it was also aired on television.

Riley's First Date? expands on the teenage boy, Jordan, seen briefly at the end of *Inside Out* and shows him meeting Riley's parents when he takes Riley skating. Josh Cooley, one of the writers of the screenplay of *Inside Out*, wrote and directed the short. He said, "I treated *Riley's First Date?* as if you were just watching more of *Inside Out*."[36] It premiered in 2015 at the D23 Expo, an event for D23: The Official Disney Fan Club and was included in the home entertainment release of *Inside Out*.

1

Mike's New Car, directed by Pete Docter and Roger Gould, shows Sulley accidentally destroying Mike's brand-new vehicle. This was the first Pixar short to feature dialogue. It appeared on the home entertainment release of *Monsters, Inc.* in 2002 and was nominated for an Academy Award for Best Animated Short Film.

After making *Ratatouille*, Pixar's filmmakers were experts on rats, and decided to show off their knowledge in *Your Friend the Rat*. In a variety of animation styles, including computer-generated, traditional hand-drawn, and stop-motion, Remy and Emile present a fact-filled lecture on their maligned species – from a rat's perspective. This short film was included with the home entertainment release of *Ratatouille* in 2007.

One other way to extend a film is with outtakes, which run during the film's end credits. They feature characters apparently forgetting their lines or making mistakes, as if they were real actors, delighting cinema audiences. *A Bug's Life* was the first film to include outtakes and they include such moments as Hopper forgetting his lines and Flik goofing around. *Toy Story 2* and *Monsters, Inc.* were two other films that featured outtakes in their end credits.

2

KEY TO PLATE

1: A car for a monster
In *Mike's New Car*, "the car itself became the centrepiece," according to co-director Roger Gould. In the monster world, the car must fit the monster: the seat adjust alone would need to allow for monsters of different shapes and sizes. "Those were the kinds of things we could go berserk with," noted Gough. Pencil drawing on paper by Gary Schultz.

2: Forky Asks a Question
Forky was created for feature film *Toy Story 4* before appearing in his own animated web series entitled *Forky Asks a Question*. In these Pixar shorts, Forky questions the other toys, many of whom belonged to Andy and Bonnie, about concepts he doesn't understand. He asks everything from "What is Love?" and "What is Art?" to "What is a Pet?" and "What is Cheese?" Digital art by Albert Lozano.

1: **Sullivan and Boo**

In *Monsters Inc.*, "Sullivan's design evolved over two years of development", according to director Pete Docter. "Boo went through several story changes as well. At various times she was a spoiled brat, a tomboy, and an eight-year-old boy" before becoming a two-year-old girl. Concept art in marker and coloured pencil by Jill Culton.

SECTION 8

A WEALTH OF DETAIL

Each Pixar film is the result of painstaking work by teams of animators and artists – from concept art and model making to the incredible blink-and-you'll-miss-them details in every final frame.

TITLE SEQUENCES AND END CREDITS

Some of the title sequences and end credits in Pixar films could be considered short films in their own right. They certainly have a visual style of their own, and although the hallmark of Pixar films is computer animation, many of these sequences have been animated in a variety of 2D styles.

In 2001, *Monsters, Inc.* set the tone with animator and illustrator Geefwee Boedoe's colourful 2D title sequence. An homage to the classic animated openings of many mid-century films, Boedoe's sequence features a fluid dance of doors, monster mouths, and slithering serpents, with a lively theme by Randy Newman.

WALL·E concluded with an ambitious end credit sequence directed by Jim Capobianco. The sequence shows how the returning humans rebuild life on Earth, using a progression of art styles from cave paintings and Ancient Egyptian scrolls to Roman mosaics and Impressionism. Capobianco said, "Unlike our credits in the past, the main goal of the credits was to finish the story. To communicate that the humans were going to be OK. They would survive."[37]

The Incredibles wraps up with an evocative 2D end credit sequence inspired by classic 1960s superheroes, created by character designer Teddy Newton.

KEY TO PLATE

1: ***WALL·E***
The end credit sequence for *WALL·E* by John Lee features many art styles including Pointillism and Post-Impressionism. The final section even references early 8-bit videogame art.

2: **Monsters, Inc.**
Geefwee Boedoe's collage concept art for the *Monsters, Inc.* title sequence.

3: **Ka-pow!**
The graphic 1960s-inspired end credits sequence for *The Incredibles* are "a two-dimensional expression of the three dimensions that are in the actual film," according to Director of Photography Andrew Jimenez. Digital artwork by Andrew Jimenez and Teddy Newton.

1

2

3

INCREDIBLE GRAPHICS

Pixar movies are rich with incidental details that make each scene feel fully realised and believable, from the book spines on the shelves to dog-eared posters hanging on bedroom walls.

All of these elements are painstakingly created, often including an incredible level of detail. In *Toy Story*, Andy's childhood drawings are pinned up on his bedroom walls, and the books on his bookcase make reference to Pixar's earlier short films *Tin Toy*, *Red's Dream*, and *Knick Knack*. In *Finding Nemo*, the dentist's waiting room is complete with well thumbed magazines, including a comic book featuring Mr Incredible from *The Incredibles*, which had not yet been released at that time.

For *Toy Story 2*, Pixar's artists created a wealth of retro-themed artworks for Woody's Roundup – including vintage cereal packets, toy commercials, board games, toy packaging, standees, and much more.

Bob's den in *The Incredibles* was also richly decorated with artwork. For *Up*, the artists crafted an array of Muntz memorabilia, as well as many monster-themed textbooks and MU College pennants for *Monsters University*.

KEY TO PLATE

1 and 2: ***Bob's den***
Many unique pieces of graphic art were created to line the walls of Bob Parr's den in *The Incredibles*. (1) Digital art by Mark Holmes and Glenn Kim. (2) Digital art by Mark Holmes.

3: ***Ellie's adventure book***
For Ellie Fredricksen's childhood journal in *Up*, the filmmakers asked director Pete Docter's daughter Elie to create some of the drawings and handwriting. "We were basically trying to get that naive childhood spirit into the book. She did a really beautiful job. No adult could have done this," said Harley Jessup. Drawing and lettering by Elie Docter, binding by Erik Evans, graphics by Craig Foster, art direction by Harley Jessup.

4: ***Childhood drawings***
Andy's childhood drawings on the walls of his bedroom. Art by Ralph Eggleston.

1

TIME
THE WEEKLY NEWS MAGAZINE
LIFE
OUTSTANDING CITIZENS PART II
SUPERHERO OF THE YEAR
"MR. INCREDIBLE"

2

Mister
INCREDIBLE
Official
FAN CLUB

MY
ADVENTURE
BOOK

3

To
Infinity
And
Beyond!

4

TAKING SHAPE

From time to time, the Pixar filmmakers have made sculptures of characters, sets, or props from clay or clay-like materials, in order to better visualise or develop the digital version of these elements.

Some sculptures are marked with grid points and lines, which are then transferred one by one into the computer using a digitising pen and computer software. Although this process can now be done using a scanner, physical sculptures are still important at the studio. Pixar's Supervising Technical Director, Bill Reeves, says, "We still do sculptures today. We don't do it for every character, but it's still a really good way to deal with the three-dimensional nature of these things."[38]

With traditional hand-drawn animation, the animators can draw characters from any angle. But with computer animation, the final digital models aren't as easily adjusted in this way. As Jerome Ranft, sculptor on *Cars 3*, said, "If you push it out in clay, everyone gets to look at it and there's no cheating, there's no lying."[39]

KEY TO PLATE

1: ***Yeti***
An early sculpt of the snow cone-loving Yeti, first seen in *Monsters Inc.*, made in cast urethane resin by Jerome Ranft.

2: ***Castle DunBroch***
For the design of Castle DunBroch in *Brave*, the team were influenced by a variety of cultures, including the Celts and Vikings. Clay and wood sculpture by Nelson Bohol.

3: ***The Parr Family***
Kent Melton's cast urethane sculpts, such as these, were referenced by the animators on *The Incredibles*.

4: ***Joy and Sadness***
Character art director Albert Lozano said, "On *Inside Out*, I didn't even touch anything digital. I would always draw with paper, pencil, with watercolours… I even did paper sculpts."

1

2

3

4

UNTIL THE VERY END

Each Pixar film starts with an idea for a story that excites and intrigues the filmmakers. Pete Docter said of his own process, "It might be a concept, a random joke, a new technique, a feeling, some experience I've gone through in my life... anything is fair game, and there are no rules."

To develop a story idea, visual development and concept artists create images to inspire the filmmakers and capture the story's feel. They begin to visualise characters, environments, props, and colour palettes. External experts and collaborators are often brought in to add fresh perspectives and strengthen the story.

With a strong story concept agreed upon, a script is developed, which is then turned into a series of hand-drawn storyboards. The storyboards are revised many times during the development of a film. The director meets regularly with a 'brain trust', a group of senior creative staff, and receives candid comments on the work in progress. The storyboarding process enables the filmmakers to decide what works and what needs changing before the far more expensive process of animation begins.

Storyboards form the blueprint for the film. Even so, the story will go through countless further changes and improvements before the film is finished. For Pixar, it's always about the story, until the very end.

1

2

3

KEY TO PLATE

1: ***Storyboard***
Helen Parr (Elastigirl) in a panel from the storyboard for *Incredibles 2*. Digital art by Ted Mathot, Brian Kalin O'Connell, and Tony Fucile.

2: ***Drawing at speed***
Storyboards typically feature simplified versions of characters, because hundreds of them have to be drawn each day for a sequence. The storyboard artists learn to draw at great speed. Storyboard frame from *Toy Story 3* by Mark Andrews.

3: ***Pitching a storyboard***
A caricature of one of the *Toy Story* co-writers pitching a storyboard. Art by Kelly Asbury, colour by Tia W. Kratter.

1

1: ***College library***

A visualisation of the impressive college library from *Monsters University*. Digital artwork by Robert Kondo.

SECTION 9

LIBRARY

INDEX
REFERENCES

INDEX

REFERENCES

1 Paik, K. 2007. *To Infinity and Beyond! The Story of Pixar Animation Studios*. San Francisco: Chronicle Books, pp. 21.
2 Paik, K. 2007, pp. 167.
3 Ibid, pp. 43.
4 Ibid, pp. 43.
5 Ibid, pp. 83.
6 Ibid, pp. 99.
7 Ibid, pp. 90.
8 Ibid, pp. 142.
9 Ibid, pp. 184.
10 Paik, K. 2013. *The Art of Monsters University*. San Francisco: Chronicle Books, pp. 7.
11 Hauser, T. 2008. *The Art of WALL•E*. San Francisco: Chronicle Books, pp. 11.
12 Robinson, T. 2008. "Andrew Stanton." The A.V. Club, 26 June. Available at: web.archive.org/web/20080908045321/avclub.com/content/interview/andrew_stanton
13 2015. Inside Out Press Kit, pp. 3.
14 Poehler, A. and Docter, P. 2015. *The Art of Inside Out*. San Francisco: Chronicle Books, pp. 7.
15 Lasseter, J. 2017. *The Art of Coco*. San Francisco: Chronicle Books, pp. 7.
16 Romano, N. 2019. "Pixar bares its *Soul* in first look at film with Jamie Foxx and Tina Fey." Entertainment Weekly, 6 November. Available at: ew.com/movies/2019/11/06/pixar-soul-photo-jamie-foxx-tina-fey/
17 Ibid, pp. 118.
18 Ibid, pp. 125.
19 Paik, K. 2007, pp. 212.
20 Lasseter, J., Pilcher. S., et al. 2016. *The Art of Finding Dory*. San Francisco: Chronicle Books, pp. 9.
21 Hauser, T. 2009. *The Art of Up*. San Francisco: Chronicle Books, pp. 7.
22 Lesnick, S. 2015. "The Good Dinosaur Story: Behind the Scenes at Pixar." ComingSoon.net, 8 October. Available at: comingsoon.net/movies/features/620701-the-good-dinosaur-story#/slide/1
23 Variety Staff. 2017. "D23: Pixar Announces Untitled Quest Movie Set in 'Suburban Fantasy World'" Variety, July 14. Available at: variety.com/2017/film/news/pixar-disney-untitled-suburban-fantasy-world-unicorns-d23-1202496455/
24 Nash, B. 2019. "With *Onward*, Pixar Once Again Wants To Help Us Find Magic In Our Everyday Lives." GQ, 3 June. Available at: gq.com.au/entertainment/film-tv/with-onward-pixar-once-again-wants-to-help-us-find-magic-in-our-everyday-lives/news-story/59d11be6bc6faa1a93e9bd0fef188ce9
25 Bell, C. 2017. "Pixar's new 'Suburban Fantasy' Sounds Like a Real Tearjerker." MTV News, 17 July. Available at: mtv.com/news/3025627/pixar-suburban-fantasy-film-dan-scanlon/
26 Falcone, D.R. 2019. "See Chris Pratt, Julia Louis-Dreyfus & Tom Holland as Elves in Disney-Pixar's *Onward*: First Look!" People, 29 May 29. Available at: people.com/movies/chris-pratt-julia-louis-dreyfus-tom-holland-onward/
27 Paik, K. 2007, pp. 236.
28 Ibid, pp. 245.
29 Ibid, pp. 267.
30 Ibid, pp. 12.
31 Lerew, J. 2012. *The Art of Brave*. San Francisco: Chronicle Books, pp. 8.
32 Grater, Tom. 2020. "Pixar Unveils Italy-Set Coming Of Age Story 'Luca' From 'La Luna' Director & 'Lava' Producer." Deadline, July 30. Available at: https://deadline.com/2020/07/pixar-to-make-italy-set-coming-of-age-story-luca-with-la-luna-director-lava-producer-1202999431/
33 Travis, Ben. 2021. "*Luca*: The Inspiration Behind Pixar's Mythical Coming-Of-Age Adventure – Exclusive Image." Empire, January 18. Available at: https://www.empireonline.com/movies/news/luca-pixar-mythical-coming-of-age-exclusive-image/
34 Inside Pixar, 2020. Deanna Marsigliese: The Art of the Pivot.
35 Deitchman, B. 2019. "You Have to Meet Purl, the Star of Pixar's Newest Short." D23, 4 February. Available at: https://d23.com/you-have-to-meet-purl-the-star-of-pixars-newest-short/
36 McKittrick, C. 2016. "'Is this the best story we can tell?' – *Inside Out*" Creative Screenwriting, 16 February. Available at: creativescreenwriting.com/is-this-the-best-story-we-can-tell-inside-out/
37 Ulloa, A. and Albinson, I. 2009. "WALL•E." Art of the Title, 22 June. Available at: artofthetitle.com/title/walle/
38 Fails, I. 2019. "Some Of Your Favorite CG 'Toy Story' Characters Actually Began As Clay Sculpts." Befores & Afters, 6 November. Available at: beforesandafters.com/2019/11/06/some-of-your-favorite-cg-toy-story-characters-actually-began-as-clay-sculpts/
39 Grafman, J. "Pixar's Clay Sculptor Shapes the World." AutoDesignO. Available at: autodesigno.com/pixars-clay-sculptor-shapes-the-world-pt-1/